Table of Contents

Alabama	1
Alaska	2
Arizona	3
Arkansas	4
California	5
Colorado	6
Connecticut	7
Delaware	8
Florida	9
Georgia	10
Hawaii	11
Idaho	12
Illinois	13
Indiana	14
Iowa	15
Kansas	16
Kentucky	17
Louisiana	18
Maine	19
Maryland	20
Massachusetts	21
Michigan	22
Minnesota	23
Mississippi	24
Missouri	25
Montana	26
Nebraska	27
Nevada	28
New Hampshire	29
New Jersey	30
New Mexico	31
New York	32
North Carolina	33
North Dakota	34
Ohio	35
Oklahoma	36
Oregon	37
Pennsylvania	38
Rhode Island	39
South Carolina	40
South Dakota	41
Tennessee	42
Texas	43
Utah	44
Vermont	45
Virginia	46
Washington	47
West Virginia	48
Wisconsin	49
Wyoming	50
Washington, D.C.	51
U.S. Dependencies—Caribbean	52
U.S. Dependencies—Pacific	53
United States Map	54
U.S. Dependencies Map	55
Answer Key	56

Introduction

The purpose of *50 States* is to help students learn more about each of the states. Each page lists questions that, when answered, will fit into one of five types of puzzles. Students will often need to do some additional searching, which will lead them to more information and photographs that will bring the landscapes, history, and people "to life."

Space places limitations on the amount that can be included on each state. However, enough about the geography, history, entertainment, agriculture, industries, tourist attractions, natural wonders, and other pertinent subjects are included to give students an appropriate overview of the state. The official state flowers and state birds are noted on the activity sheets. Encourage students to bring and display pictures of these state symbols.

It is important to note that with all racial and cultural groups, one should be sensitive to the use of terms that are preferred in their part of the country. For example, in this book, the term Indian is often used. Native peoples are referred to as Native Americans, as Indians, or by tribal affiliation. Particular terms are more appropriate in some areas than in others.

The U.S. Dependencies are divided into Pacific and Caribbean regions. The questions in this book will give students a basic understanding of what a dependency is, but they may wish to do additional research so each one emerges with its own identity.

It is hoped the students will enjoy the challenge of the research needed to solve the puzzles, will learn a lot about each state, and will be motivated to want to learn even more. It would be especially nice if they developed a desire to travel the country someday, learning about the uniqueness of each region and also the similarities that bind us together into one strong country.

★ 50 States ★

by Lynda Hatch

illustrated by Milton Hall

cover design by Jeff Van Kanegan

Publisher
Instructional Fair • TS Denison
Grand Rapids, Michigan 49544

About the Author

Lynda Hatch is the Coordinator of Elementary Education at Northern Arizona University's Center for Excellence in Education in Flagstaff. She does educational consulting throughout the United States and around the world. Lynda also writes extensively for teachers and children. In Oregon and Washington, she was a classroom teacher and curriculum specialist. In 1982, she was Oregon's Teacher of the Year and is listed in *Who's Who in American Education.*

Instructional Fair • TS Denison grants the individual purchaser permission to reproduce the student activity materials in this book for noncommercial individual or classroom use only. Reproduction for an entire school or school system is strictly prohibited. No part of this publication may be reproduced for storage in a retrieval system, or transmitted in any form or by any means, electronic, mechanical, recording, or otherwise, without the prior written permission of the publisher. For information regarding permission, write to Instructional Fair • TS Denison, P.O. Box 1650, Grand Rapids, MI 49501.

ISBN: 1-56822-457-5
50 States
Copyright © 1997 by Instructional Fair • TS Denison
2400 Turner Avenue NW
Grand Rapids, Michigan 49544

All Rights Reserved • Printed in the USA

Yellow hammer Heart of Dixie Camellia

Place the answers to the questions in the crossword puzzle.

Across

2. _____ T. Washington founded Tuskegee Institute (now university) in 1881, mainly as a black college. He recruited black botanist, George Washington Carver, to teach and do research here. Carver developed over 300 products from peanuts, such as ink, soap, and shaving cream. He also developed products from sweet potatoes and soybeans.
6. _____ is called "Rocket City, USA" because it is a center for space research. Rockets such as the *Saturn V,* which launched *Apollo 11* carrying the first astronauts to land on the moon, were made here.
7. Visitors to ____ Cave National Monument in Bridgeport can see where people lived 10,000 years ago. Archeologists have studied the many layers of refuse that were left behind by people for 8,000 years. It has not decomposed.
8. Alabama is known as the "Heart of ____." During Civil War days, the Confederate Constitution was developed here. Montgomery was the first Confederate capital and the headquarters of Jefferson Davis, the Confederate President.

Down

1. Alabama is rich in iron ore, limestone, and coal. These are used to make iron and steel. Since Birmingham is close to these deposits, it became an iron and steel-making center. Sloss _____ National Historic Landmark is a museum about iron making. Not as much iron and steel is made in Birmingham today.
2. Alabama's Black Belt region is in the middle of the state. In earlier days, this was the site of large cotton plantations. Cotton was planted, picked, and cleaned by slaves. At first, it was thought to be a disaster when the _____ weevil chewed its way through the crop. This bug was really a blessing. Peanuts were planted as an alternative crop and became even more profitable.
3. About 1,000 years ago, Alabama's Indians built large dirt _____. On top of some were buildings. Others contained graves. Many can be seen at the archeological park in Moundville.
4. Alabama has been the site of much of the civil rights history in the United States. In 1955, Rosa Parks, a tired black woman, refused to give up her seat in the "whites only" part of a Montgomery bus. Martin Luther King, Jr., led protests against her arrest. In 1965, King led a march from _____ to Montgomery, protesting that many blacks could not vote. In 1963, Governor Wallace tried to keep black students from attending the University of Alabama. These injustices were found to be illegal and were changed.
5. Helen _____ lost her sight and hearing as a young child in Tuscumbia. She learned to read, write, and speak from her tutor, Anne Sullivan. She wrote many books, showed the capabilities of the physically challenged, and paved the way for others to be educated.
7. The state has beautiful and varied scenery. The north is famous for its _____ clay soils. The state also has pine forests, rolling grasslands, swamps, and white sandy beaches.

© Instructional Fair • TS Denison   1   IF2736 50 States

Willow ptarmigan

The Last Frontier

Forget-me-not

Write the letter from Column B that most correctly answers the description found in Column A. Note: More choices are given in Column B than will be used for answers.

Column A

____ 1. Most northerly city in the United States, where the sun does not set for three months in summer and does not rise for two months in winter

____ 2. Alaska's native peoples include the Aleuts, the Northwest Coast Indians such as the Tlingit and Haida tribes, several Athapaskan tribes, and this major group of people.

____ 3. William Seward, U.S. Secretary of State, bought Alaska from this country in 1867 for 2 cents an acre, even though many people thought Alaska was a wasteland.

____ 4. This mineral was discovered in 1896, causing many people to rush to Alaska to seek their riches.

____ 5. One of the largest construction jobs in history built this from Prudhoe Bay to Valdez to carry oil to port.

____ 6. Snowmobiles and airplanes have replaced the need for dogsleds, but this dogsled race is very popular in Alaska.

____ 7. Mt. McKinley, the tallest peak in North America at 20,320', is in this national park.

____ 8. Native people carved these, not to worship them, but to tell a legend, history, or be a family crest. The largest collection can be seen in Ketchikan.

____ 9. This industry is larger in Alaska than in any other state. Big factories keep busy freezing and canning salmon, crabs, halibut, and shrimp, as fast as the boats bring in the catch.

____ 10. These curtains, bands, and ribbons of colorful lights in the night sky occur when charged particles from the sun bang into the earth's atmosphere.

Column B
A. Denali National Park
B. Anchorage
C. Iditarod
D. Totem poles
E. Gold
F. Pribilof Islands
G. Point Barrow
H. Trans-Alaska Pipeline
I. Aurora borealis
J. Glacier Bay National Monument
K. Fisheries
L. Capt. James Cook
M. Eskimos
N. Russia
O. Forestry
P. Canada
Q. Joe Juneau
R. Mendenhall Glacier
S. Aleutian Islands

Cactus wren

Grand Canyon State

Saguaro cactus flower

Fill in the lines with the answers to the questions. Then arrange the answers to fit into the puzzle boxes.

1. Observatory where planet Pluto was discovered and where the theory of the "expanding universe" was formed
   _____

2. Giant cactus that grows slowly in the Sonoran Desert, taking 25 years to grow just two feet tall
   _____

3. Important crop that was introduced from Egypt to grow in the hot climate of the Salt River Valley
   _____

4. Largest city, named for the mythological bird which was destroyed by fire and rose from its own ashes, much like this city built on the ruins of the ancient Hohokam civilization
   _____

5. The "town too tough to die," famous for the Gunfight at O.K. Corral between U.S. Marshal Wyatt Earp, Doc Holliday, and the Clanton Gang
   _____

6. Giant hole in the ground, probably formed when 60,000 tons of iron and nickel hit the earth about 22,000 years ago, which became a training site for astronauts preparing for moon walks (two words)
   _____

7. Largest of the 14 Native American tribes located in the state, famous for their woven rugs and silver jewelry
   _____

8. Formed 200 million years ago when a large lake covered a forested valley and the minerals in the water seeped into the trees, turning them to stone (two words)
   _____

9. One of the earth's most spectacular sights, showing colorful rock layers, formed by millions of years of water erosion of the Colorado River (two words)
   _____

10. Purchased in London, England, and shipped piece-by-piece and reconstructed as a tourist attraction at Lake Havasu City (two words)
    _____

© Instructional Fair • TS Denison

3

IF2736 50 States

Mockingbird   **Land of Opportunity**   Apple blossom

Fill in the lines with the answers to the questions. Then arrange the answers to fit into the puzzle boxes.

_____ 1. These fictitious animals were said to be wild hogs with such sharp ridges on their backs that men shaved with them. These animals are now the team mascot of the University of Arkansas.

_____ 2. The only mine of its kind in the United States operated from 1908-1925. Now, visitors can dig this gem at a state park near Murfreesboro.

_____ 3. The name of Arkansas came from the French pronunciation of this tribe of Sioux Indians.

_____ 4. This Arkansas native commanded the Allied Forces in the Pacific during World War II and accepted Japan's surrender, which ended the war.

_____ 5. This high school in Little Rock became well-known in 1957 when President Eisenhower had to send federal troops to enforce the integration of black students into a formerly all-white school.

_____ 6. The mountains where arts and crafts of the 1800s, such as candles, baskets, quilts, and applehead and cornhusk dolls, are demonstrated at a folk center at Mountain View.

_____ 7. These are grown near Hope, which is the site of the annual festival where prizes are given for the largest, generally weighing over 200 pounds.

_____ 8. When these creatures are only nine weeks old, they become the state's number one farm product. The main center for their production is near Springdale.

_____ 9. This national park is known for its soothing water that is piped into large indoor pools, where people come to soak aching joints and tired muscles (two words).

_____ 10. This beautiful free-flowing river in the Ozarks has been named a national river, so it is protected from being dammed or having its banks developed.

© Instructional Fair • TS Denison   4   IF2736 50 States

★ CALIFORNIA ★

California valley quail   **Golden State**   Golden poppy

Fill in the answers to the following questions. A few clues are given.

1. This national park is known for its gigantic granite walls with names like El Capitan and Half Dome. It also has deep canyons, spectacular waterfalls, peaks, rivers, and valleys.   _ _ _ _ M _(_)_

2. This physical feature of California has the lowest elevation in North America, 282' below sea level. It gets only about 2" of rain a year. Despite its name, it is home to many plants and animals.   (_)_ _ _ _ _(_)_ L _ _ _

3. This event began when a workman at Sutter's sawmill near Sacramento discovered gold in 1848.   _ _ _ _ _(_)S _ _

4. During the Pleistocene period, over 200 types of animals, such as saber-tooth cats and mastadons, were trapped in these tar pits in Los Angeles.   _(_) _(_)E_

5. California has world record-setting trees. The largest sequoia is 102' around. The tallest redwood is 362'. This type of pine is the oldest tree, dating back 4,600 years.   _ _ _ _ _ _ C _ _(_)

6. Starting in 1769 with Padre Junípero Serra, the Spanish established a chain of 21 of these along El Camino Real. They hoped to convert the Indians to Christianity and teach them to live in the Spanish culture.   _ _ S _ _ _(_)_

7. This valley is the region between San Jose and Redwood City that produces much high technology. It is named after the chip, an important part of many electronic devices.   (_)_ _ _ _ _ N _

8. Many Californians work in this industry. The state is a major producer of grapes, strawberries, lettuce, tomatoes, and half the country's fruits and vegetables.   (_)_ I _(_)_ _

9. This peninsula is known for its scenic coastal Seventeen-Mile Drive, historic Cannery Row shops, outstanding aquarium, and the galleries, boutiques, and beach of Carmel.   _ _(_)T _ _ _ _

10. This interesting city is popular with tourists who ride cable cars and visit the Golden Gate Bridge, Alcatraz, Chinatown, Nob Hill, and Fisherman's Wharf.   _(_)_ (_)_ _ _ C _(_)_

Write the letters found in the circles. Unscramble these letters until they provide the answer to the name of the place where plates deep in the earth's crust move, causing many California earthquakes.

_ _ _   _ _ _ _ _ _

© Instructional Fair • TS Denison   5   IF2736 50 States

Lark bunting

Centennial State

Rocky Mountain columbine

Locate the answers to the following questions in the word search.

1. Winds have piled up North America's tallest sand _____ near Alamosa for thousands of years, making some of them 700' tall, the height of a 70-story building.

2. An atomic clock, the most accurate in the country, is in Boulder, at the National Bureau of _____, the agency that decides the country's exact time and exact weights.

3. Bent's Old _____ near La Junta, established in 1833-1834, was Colorado's first permanent non-Indian settlement, which was established as a trading post.

4. Western Colorado was home to over 50 kinds of dinosaurs, including tyrannosaurus rex, stegosaurus, brachiosaurus, and apatosaurus, at what is today _____ National Monument, in both Colorado and Utah.

5. Colorado Springs is the home of the United States Olympic Training Complex, Pro Rodeo Hall of Fame, World Figure Skating Hall of Fame, Garden of the Gods, and the U.S. Air Force _____.

6. _____ Mountain National Park near Estes Park is a scenic area of peaks, meadows, canyons, lakes, streams, and thousands of miles of hiking trails.

7. Mining has been important to Colorado, with gold discovered at Cherry Creek (Denver) in 1858, silver found in 1878 in Aspen and Leadville, another _____ rush in 1890 in Cripple Creek, and then oil ("black gold") discovered in the early 1900s.

8. The largest site of ancient Indian cliff dwellings in the world is found at Mesa Verde National Park near Cortez, an 800-year-old _____ site which was active with people from about 500 B.C. to A.D. 1300.

9. Over five billion coins, with the letter "D" for Denver on them, are minted each year at the Denver _____, one of only three other federal mints in the United States.

10. _____ Peak near Colorado Springs, one of Colorado's most famous mountains, was where Katherine Lee Bates was inspired by the scenery in 1893 and wrote a poem that was later set to music and became "America the Beautiful."

```
C R O Y M E D A C A S D
O B O U S B V T A D U E
N E T C E J E T R I A N
T A E G K S R A R N I V
I D O M I Y D O E O R E
N L U I P N E A R S F R
E O A N A S A Z I A A R
N G O T E M E S A U N U
T E S F O S S I L R C S
A D U R A N G O A L E H
```

Robin

Constitution State

Mountain laurel

Place the answers to the questions in the crossword puzzle.

Across

4. In 1662, the King of England gave Connecticut Colony a charter which allowed the colonists more control of their government and gave them land. When a new king ruled, he wanted more control of the colonies and demanded the charter back. Connecticut's leaders hid it in the hollow of an old oak tree. This became known as the Charter _____ and was a symbol for Connecticut's love of freedom.
5. _____ Seaport is a reconstructed nineteenth-century whaling village where tourists can get a feel for history.
6. Nathan _____ was a Connecticut teacher and Revolutionary War hero. Before he was hanged by the British for spying, he said, "I only regret that I have but one life to lose for my country."
8. Connecticut's state song is _____. It is said that Connecticut volunteers leaving to help the British in the French and Indian War were given chicken feathers to substitute for plumes in their makeshift uniform hats. When they arrived, the British surgeon said, "They're macaronies!" which was slang for an overdressed person. He put it in a poem which became a song. (two words)
10. _____ University in New Haven is one of the oldest in the country. It runs the Peabody Museum of Natural History, which has a large collection of dinosaur fossils.

Down

1. Connecticut has a long history of _____. Factories make many submarines, helicopters, and jet engines.
2. Connecticut had the first commercial _____ switchboard in the United States, first installed in New Haven in 1878. It also had the first phone book.
3. Hartford is the _____ capital of the world. Many companies have headquarters in Connecticut, which started with the Hartford Fire Insurance Company in 1794.
7. Harriet Beecher _____ was born in Litchfield. Her book *Uncle Tom's Cabin* helped turn people against slavery.
9. Thomas Gallaudet and Laurent Clerc founded the first school for the _____ in the United States in Hartford in 1817.

© Instructional Fair • TS Denison   7   IF2736 50 States

Blue hen chicken

First State

Peach blossom

Place the answers to the questions in the crossword puzzle.

Across
1. During the Revolutionary War, Captain Caldwell's company raised blue hen chickens. It was popular at this time for people to raise chickens to _____ each other. These birds were so fierce, just like the Delaware soldiers, that the soldiers also became known as Blue Hen Chickens. The chickens became the mascots of the soldiers.
5. It is said that a cargo ship carrying peas was wrecked on a sandbar, spilling the peas into the river. The peas sprouted and got caught in the sand, forming an island known as Pea _____ Island. Today it is the site of Fort Delaware State Park.
9. Delaware's legislature passed the Delaware _____ Law in 1899, which made it easy for people to form companies in the state. Other states had stricter rules and higher taxes for companies. Many companies did their business in other states but paid taxes in Delaware. This made the state very rich and has continued to bring new business to Delaware.
10. In 1974, Dr. Henry J. Heimlich, a native of Wilmington, invented a way to help people who are choking. His Heimlich _____ has saved thousands of lives.

Down
2. In 1799, the Du Pont Family settled in Delaware from France. They started a successful company which made _____. Later, they became known for their chemical research and manufacturing. They produced nylon, the first synthetic (man-made) fiber. Today, they also make chemical products such as Teflon, cellophane, polyester, Dacron, and Orlon.
3. Delaware was the _____ state to ratify (approve) the U.S. Constitution. It was signed on December 7, 1787.
4. Delaware was named after Lord De La Warr, the _____ of Virginia, by an English sea captain who, in 1610, mistakenly sailed into what became known as Delaware Bay.
6. On September 3, 1777, the _____ flag was displayed in battle for the first time. This was in the Revolutionary War Battle of Cooch's Bridge, the only battle of this war fought in Delaware.
7. A group of Swedish settlers built the first log _____ in America at Fort Christina in 1638. This became the first permanent settlement in Delaware. The Dutch and English were also early European settlers. Delaware is the only state to have had three European flags fly over its original colony, the Dutch, Swedish, and English.
8. In 1923, Cecile Steele started a new business for Delaware. On her farm she raised broiler _____. These animals are between 9–12 weeks old and are raised for their meat. This has become a very large industry for Delaware.

© Instructional Fair • TS Denison
IF2736 50 States

Mockingbird   **Sunshine State**   Orange blossom

Fill in the answers to the following questions. A few clues are given.

1. Although most of these Indians were moved to Oklahoma in 1842, some still live in Florida. The tribe was formed by Creek refugees, members of other tribes, and escaped slaves.
2. These islands are located off the southern tip of Florida. Key West was the home of many writers, including Ernest Hemingway.
3. There are about 1,000 of these gentle animals, also known as sea cows, in Florida. They are a protected species.
4. This city is the home to many immigrants who escaped from Communist Cuba. They have had a big influence on food, language, and politics.
5. This is a large industry in Florida because of the sunshine, warm ocean, and attractions such as Walt Disney World.
6. This city is the first permanent European settlement in North America.
7. Florida is the leader in the nation in producing this type of crop. The Spanish first brought oranges to St. Augustine.
8. This national park is a large subtropical wilderness. It is composed of swampy grasslands with unusual plants and animals such as alligators, cougars, and bald eagles.
9. This city got its name because of a shipwreck. In 1878, the *Providencia* sank. Its cargo of coconuts washed ashore, took root, and the city was named for them.
10. This Spanish explorer searched unsuccessfully for the Fountain of Youth in 1513. He named the land Florida because of arriving during Pascua Florida, or "Flowery Easter."

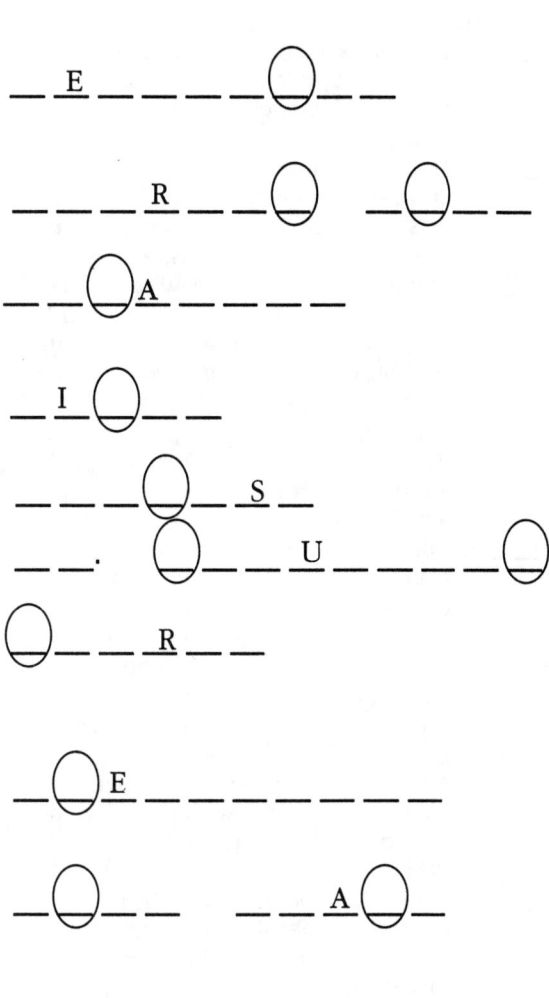

Write the letters found in the circles. Unscramble these letters until they provide the answer to the name of the home of the Kennedy Space Center and main launch site for U.S. space exploration, near Cocoa Beach.

_ _ _ _   _ _ _ _ _ _ _ _ _

Brown thrasher

★ GEORGIA ★
Empire State of the South

Cherokee rose

Write the letter from Column B that most correctly answers the description found in Column A. Note: More choices are given in Column B than will be used for answers.

Column A

___ 1. First black man, from Cairo, allowed to play major league baseball. He was later inducted into the Baseball Hall of Fame.

___ 2. Georgia is the leading state for this crop, also known as goobers, which was the crop raised by President Jimmy Carter from Plains.

___ 3. Town where the "Little White House" is located where President Franklin D. Roosevelt came to bathe in nearby healthful mineral springs after he got polio, and where he died.

___ 4. Minister, born in Atlanta, who made the famous "I Have a Dream" speech and who won the Nobel Peace Prize for civil rights leadership

___ 5. Author, born in Atlanta, who wrote *Gone with the Wind*, a famous book (and movie) about life in the South during the Civil War period

___ 6. Started Girl Guides in the United States in 1912 (later called Girl Scouts), which had originated in England

___ 7. Author, sometimes referred to as "Georgia's Aesop," who recorded the tales of Uncle Remus and Br'er Rabbit

___ 8. Three Confederate Civil War heroes, Generals Robert E. Lee, Jefferson Davis, and Stonewall Jackson, are carved out of this mountain, the world's largest isolated block of granite.

___ 9. This 681-square-mile swamp, in southeast Georgia and northern Florida, has spongy mats of plant life that look like islands and shiver when walked on.

___10. Inventor of the cotton gin in 1793 which helped the industry, making the cleaning of cotton 50 times faster than a person cleaning it by hand

Column B

A. Joel Chandler Harris
B. James Ogelthorpe
C. Okefenokee
D. Margaret Mitchell
E. Jackie Robinson
F. Atlanta
G. Peanuts
H. Eli Whitney
I. New Echota
J. Juliette Gordon Low
K. Andrew Young
L. Warm Springs
M. Stone Mountain
N. Martin Luther King, Jr.
O. Appalachian Trail
P. Cumberland Island National Seashore
Q. Rabun Gap
R. Ty Cobb
S. Ocmulgee National Monument

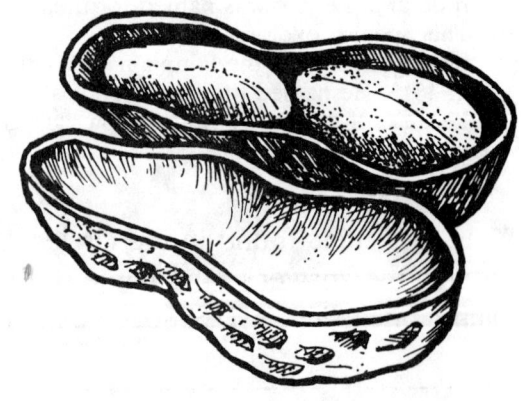

© Instructional Fair • TS Denison   10   IF2736 50 States

Nene (Hawaiian goose)

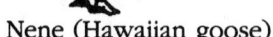
Aloha State

Hibiscus

Locate the answers to the following questions in the word search.

1. _____ is a major industry, because visitors come to Hawaii for its mild climate and the natural beauty of blue seas, flowers, palm trees, waterfalls, sandy beaches, coral reefs, and lush mountain scenery.
2. In 1778, Englishman Captain _____ Cook discovered Hawaii for Europeans but upset the natives by eating too much of their food. In a fight, Cook and four of his crew were killed. But soon other European ships arrived, changing Hawaii forever.
3. The warm weather and wet environment is ideal for the growing of subtropical crops such as sugar cane and pineapples, which are farmed on large _____ that need many workers.
4. Hawaii is the only state to have been a monarchy, starting with King _____, who conquered all of the islands by 1810. The last monarch was Queen Liliuokalani, who was overthrown by U.S. troops in 1893, ending the Kingdom of Hawaii and beginning the Republic of Hawaii, leading to Hawaii becoming a U.S. Territory in 1900 and the fiftieth state in 1959.
5. The Kulaupapa Peninsula of Molokai was home to exiled Hawaiians who had Hansen's Disease, or _____, and without help, thousands died in the 1800s. Eventually, they were helped by Father Damien Joseph de Veuster, a Catholic priest who eventually died of the disease himself.
6. The United States entered World War II after Honolulu's Pearl Harbor Navy Base and _____ Air Force Base were attacked by the Japanese on December 7, 1941, destroying many ships and planes and killing 2,500 Americans. These people are now honored at the USS *Arizona* National Memorial, built over the submerged battleship *Arizona*.
7. The 132 Hawaiian Islands, 8 of which are inhabited—Niihau, Kauai, Oahu, Molokai, Lanai, Maui, Hawaii (Big Island), and Kahoolawe—are the peaks of huge underwater volcanoes and can be studied at Hawaii Volcanoes National Park on the Big Island and _____ National Park on Maui.
8. Hawaiians invented _____ and were already holding contests when Europeans first arrived in the 1700s. It remains a popular sport because of the huge waves on several coasts.
9. The original Hawaiians were _____ who sailed to Hawaii from the Marquesas Islands 2,000 years ago (and from Tahiti about 800 years later) in large canoes. Their clothing, crafts, dances, and music are shown at the Polynesian Cultural Center on Oahu.
10. The Hawaiians did not have a written language for many years, so the _____ dance was important to them. It was a way to tell their history, stories, and religion, so watching the body motions was like "reading a book."

```
H S N O I T A T N A L P Y
U I P O L Y N E S I A N S
L L C V O L C A N O M S O
A O A K L E I S J H S U R
A H E M A H E M A K I R P
S U G A R M O A H U R F E
A L A K A E L A H N U I L
L A V J M I S S I O O N K
T R Y R O T I R R E T G C
```

© Instructional Fair • TS Denison   11   IF2736 50 States

Mountain blue bird

Gem State

Idaho syringa
(mock orange)

Fill in the answers to the following questions. A few clues are given.

1. More people of this nationality live in Idaho than anywhere outside of Spain. When they first came to Idaho, they were sheepherders.
B _ _ _ _ O

2. Idaho is the number one producer of this crop.
_ _ _ A _ _ O

3. This waterfall on the Snake River is higher than Niagara Falls. Several towns are named for falls—Idaho, Twin, and American.
_ _ _ _ O o _ _ _ _ _ O

4. These were left when miners came to an area, quickly put up buildings, and then left when the riches ran out. A famous one in Idaho is Silver City, a popular tourist attraction.
_ _ _ _ T _ _ _ O _

5. This national monument is filled with volcanic lava fields, caves, tubes, and cones. It resembles the surface of the moon.
O _ _ _ _ _ _ _ F _ _ _ _

6. Idaho's capital had first been this northern Idaho town. One day a band of lawmakers rode off with the territorial seal and official papers, took them to Boise, and declared it the new capital.
_ E _ _ _ _ _ O

7. Idaho is known for its beautiful mountains. This mountain resort is popular for skiing and hiking.
_ _ _ _ _ L _ _ O

8. These famous American explorers crossed the Bitterroot Range and floated down the Clearwater and Snake Rivers. They were helped by the Shoshone Indians.
_ _ _ _ S _ _ _ _ _ O _ _ _

9. Idaho has more miles of this type of river rapids than any other state. The Salmon and Snake Rivers attract rafters to these challenging rapids.
_ _ _ _ _ _ O _ _ R

10. Idaho has many Oregon Trail ruts and sites. This reconstructed fur trading post in Pocatello also sold the pioneers supplies.
_ O _ _ _ _ _ L _

Write the letters found in the circles. Unscramble these letters until they provide the name of the deepest canyon in North America, deeper than the Grand Canyon, located where the Snake River divides the Idaho-Oregon border.

_ _ _ _ _   _ _ _ _ _ _

Cardinal

ILLINOIS
Land of Lincoln

Violet

Place the answers to the questions in the crossword puzzle.

Across

5. The nation's largest deposit of _____ coal is under ⅔ of Illinois. When this soft coal is burned, a lot of pollution is created, so it is not mined as often now.
7. *Illinois* is the French interpretation of _____, the name of the native peoples of the area. It means "the people" and is the name of the six tribes—Cahokia, Kaskaskia, Michigamea, Moingwena, Peoria, and Tamaroa.
9. The skyscraper was invented in Chicago. The Home Insurance Building was completed in 1885 as the first skyscraper. Today, one of the world's tallest buildings, Sears _____ (110 stories), is in downtown Chicago.
10. The _____ Hills in the southern part of the state is an area of lovely hills, valleys, forests, lakes, and caves. Cave-in-Rock on the Ohio River was once a pirate's hideout. Another attraction is Garden of the Gods, where rocks have been eroded into strange shapes by water and wind.

Down

1. The Mississippi River and _____ Lakes are connected in Chicago, making it an important shipping center. Part river/part canal, this water route connects the Gulf of Mexico with the Atlantic Ocean through the Great Lakes. Chicago is also a center of highway, railroad, and airplane traffic.
2. The flat prairie land with its rich soil is ideal for farming. Illinois grows a lot of corn and soybeans. The city of _____, home of John Deere and other farm machinery manufacturers, is known as the "Farm Machinery Capital of the World." Deere invented the first steel plow at Grand Detour in 1837.
3. In Illinois, _____ Lincoln practiced law, entered politics, and was nominated for president. Today, visitors can tour Lincoln's New Salem State Park to see where he lived as a young lawyer. In the 1930s, the state of Illinois rebuilt this town to look like it did when Lincoln lived there.
4. The first European exploration of the Mississippi River and Illinois was by _____ Joliet and Jacques Marquette in 1763. They were part of a French Canadian exploration and fur trapping expedition.
6. Chicago did not get its nickname, the "Windy _____," from its weather, although it does have a lot of wind. Instead, a New York City writer named it in the late 1800s. He thought people from Chicago were "windy" because they bragged so much about their city.
8. The Great Chicago Fire, which started October 8, 1871, left much of the city in ruin. People say it started when a cow kicked over a _____ in Kate O'Leary's barn. The fire burned for 31 hours, destroying nearly 20,000 buildings and killing at least 300 people.

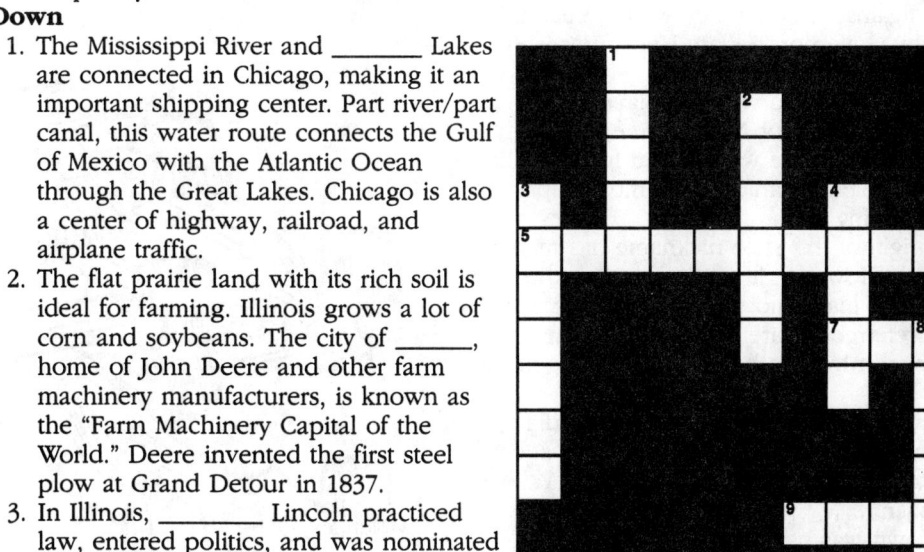

Cardinal

Hoosier State

Peony

Write the letter from Column B that most correctly answers the description found in Column A. Not all of the letters will be used.

Column A

____ 1. They are devout Christians who preserve the older traditions of farming and do not drive cars, use electricity, or go to war.

____ 2. He made horse-drawn wagons, automobiles, and wheelbarrows for gold miners in California. During World War II, he made vehicles for the military.

____ 3. He improved the cornet mouthpiece that became popular with musicians. His company eventually developed into the largest musical instrument business in the world.

____ 4. He helped slaves escape to freedom in Canada by hiding over 2,000 slaves in a secret room in his house between 1826-1847. His home in Fountain City has been saved as a monument to all who helped slaves escape.

____ 5. Every Memorial Day weekend this prestigious 500-mile, 200-lap automobile race is watched by large crowds.

____ 6. This battle occurred when two Shawnee brothers, Tecumseh and Tenskwatawa, brought many tribes together to defend their lands against settlers. They were defeated in 1811 by Governor William Henry Harrison's forces.

____ 7. He was born in Norway but played and coached football for Notre Dame University's "Fighting Irish." He was known for his belief that good sportsmanship was more important than winning.

____ 8. The origin of this state nickname has many theories. However, it may have been the name of a man who was working in Kentucky and preferred to hire his workers from across the river in Indiana because they were more reliable.

____ 9. This area is important to Indiana's wildlife because its wilderness protects plants and animals from the urban growth along Lake Michigan.

____ 10. This town was named at Christmastime in 1846. Holiday World was built as the country's first theme park with rides and a toy and doll museum.

Column B

A. Charles G. Conn
B. Northwest territory
C. Levi Coffin
D. Knute Rockne
E. Amish and Mennonites
F. Indianapolis 500
G. Tippecanoe
H. Wyandotte Cave
I. Hoosier
J. George Rogers Clark
K. Angel Mounds Memorial
L. John Studebaker
M. Santa Claus
N. Basketball
O. Indiana Dunes National Lakeshore
P. Manufacturing
Q. Abraham Lincoln
R. Ohio River
S. Corn

American goldfinch

Hawkeye State

Wild rose

Place the answers to the questions in the crossword puzzle.

Across

2. Iowa gets the greatest number of _____ of any state. There have been amazing stories of animals surviving these Iowa storms. A dairy cow became known as Fawn the Flying Cow. In two different years the storms picked up Fawn and blew her through the air and she landed unhurt.
8. One unusual group of Iowa soldiers who fought in the Civil War for the Union was nicknamed the _____. No man was under 45 years old and some were in their seventies. Some of the men had grandchildren serving in the army with them! They acted as guards for Confederate prisoners.
9. Charles Ringling was born in McGregor. He and his brothers put on circus acts in their _____. Under Charles' leadership, the brothers built the country's leading circus, the Ringling Brothers and Shrine Circus.
10. People from _____ founded the religious community of Amana. From 1885-1932, people in these seven villages communally shared all land, buildings, and machinery. The Amana Society now operates their agriculture and business operations. Visitors buy furniture, baked goods, and woolen cloth. Today they also make refrigerators, freezers, and microwave ovens.

Down

1. The state's nickname, the "_____ State," came from the Sauk Chief Black Hawk, who waged war against settlers who intruded on Indian lands in the Black Hawk War.
3. Iowa has one of the highest _____ rates in the United States. This is the ability to read and write.
4. Grant _____, of Anamosa, spent years trying to paint like European artists but had little success. Finally, he realized, "All my really good ideas came when I was milking a cow." He began to paint pictures of Iowa scenes. He then achieved great fame. His most famous painting is *American Gothic*.
5. Thousands of years ago, _____ covered much of what is now Iowa. When they melted, they left rich fertile soils and gently rolling hills, which are good for farming. Poet Robert Frost once said that Iowa's soil looked "good enough to eat."
6. Iowa produces more _____ than any place in the world. From these animals we get pork chops, bacon, sausage, and ham. Iowa leads the United States in growing corn for livestock and people.
7. Ancestors of Native Americans, known as Mound Builders, made huge dirt hills in the shape of animals and people. At _____ Mounds near Marquette, there are about 200 mounds. They are thought to be over 2,500 years old. Some are up to 300' long. Many were used as burial places.

© Instructional Fair • TS Denison   15   IF2736 50 States

Western Meadowlark   **Sunflower State**   Sunflower

Fill in the lines with the answers to the questions. Then arrange the answers to fit into the puzzle boxes.

_____ 1. Her well-known children's book, *Little House on the Prairie,* describes her experiences as a child growing up on the Kansas prairie.

_____ 2. He was raised in Abilene in a poor family but grew up to be a five-star general, led the Allied Forces in Europe during World War II, and became the thirty-fourth president of the United States.

_____ 3. This is the famous book and movie in which Dorothy, a Kansas girl, was carried off by a cyclone and spoke the well-known phrase, "There's no place like home." (four words)

_____ 4. This imaginary Kansas bird is said to have a red head and to wear yellow shoes and got its name from a term used for those who opposed slavery before the Civil War.

_____ 5. Kansas leads the nation in the production of this crop, which grows well because of fertile soil and a seed that grows well in dry climates.

_____ 6. "Cowboy Capital of the World," it was full of outlaws, shootouts, and cowboys wildly celebrating the end of the Texas cattle drives. This made it difficult for Wyatt Earp, Bat Masterson, and Wild Bill Hickok to keep the peace (two words).

_____ 7. A conflict over this issue before the Civil War led to so much violence that the area was called "Bleeding Kansas."

_____ 8. Near this town is the geodetic center of the continental United States, which government mapmakers and surveyors use as a reference point for property lines and international boundaries.

_____ 9. Wichita is the leading manufacturing center for the commercial, private, and military types of this product.

_____ 10. This lady from Atchison was the first woman to fly solo across the Atlantic Ocean. She mysteriously disappeared in the South Pacific when she tried to fly around the world in 1937.

© Instructional Fair • TS Denison   16   IF2736 50 States

Cardinal

Bluegrass State

Goldenrod

Write the letter from Column B that most correctly answers the description found in Column A.

Note: More choices are given in Column B than will be used for answers.

Column A

____ 1. His restaurant in Corbin that specialized in serving tasty fried chicken grew into a chain called Kentucky Fried Chicken (KFC).

____ 2. Thick, lush plant which has a bluish tint in spring when tiny blue flowers bloom, used to feed horses

____ 3. Frontiersman who blazed a trail called the Wilderness Road and founded the town of Boonesboro in 1767

____ 4. Steel, granite, and concrete building where the U.S. gold reserves are kept under tight security, allowing no visitors

____ 5. Thoroughbred horse race that is run at Churchill Downs each May, where the winning horse wins a blanket of roses

____ 6. This point, where Kentucky, Tennessee, and Virginia meet, was a natural route through the mountains for early Kentucky settlers and was also an important Civil War site.

____ 7. National park that has over 330 miles of underground passages and thought to be the largest in the world, formed over thousands of years by acidic water trickling through limestone.

____ 8. City called "Horse Capital of the World," in the heart of the Bluegrass region, famous for the raising of thoroughbred horses used for racing

____ 9. Natural resource that originally began to form when swamp plants died. As they decayed, heat and pressure from deposits of mud and sand slowly dried and hardened.

____10. Great songwriter who visited relatives at Bardstown. Their home inspired him to write the song, "My Old Kentucky Home."

Column B

A. Daniel Boone
B. Louisville
C. Coal
D. Mammoth Cave
E. Harland Sanders
F. Hatfields and McCoys
G. Lexington
H. Stephen Foster
I. Cumberland Gap
J. Jefferson Davis
K. Bluegrass
L. Boy Scouts of America
M. Fort Knox
N. Cumberland Falls
O. Bourbon whiskey
P. American Printing House for the Blind
Q. Kentucky Derby
R. Louisville Sluggers

© Instructional Fair • TS Denison
IF2736 50 States

Brown pelican — Pelican State — Magnolia blossom

Place the answers to the questions in the crossword puzzle.

Across

3. Jazz originated in New Orleans as a blend of black and Creole music. It was originally played at _____, starting with sad music and changing to uplifting, happy music. Famous jazz musicians include Louis Armstrong, Earl Hines, and Duke Ellington.
6. Nearly ⅓ of Louisiana is wetlands. There are swamps, marshes, bayous, rivers, and lakes, including the large _____ Pontchartrain. Wetlands are home to alligators, otters, and nutria.
8. The _____ Oak stands in St. Martinville. It was named after Henry Wadsworth Longfellow's 1847 poem. It is a poem based on a love story about the Cajun journey from Canada to Louisiana. The young lovers are separated and meet again at this oak tree.
10. Many people are descendants of the original French and _____ settlers. They are called Creoles.

Down

1. European control of Louisiana went back and forth between Spain and France several times. The state was named by the French explorer, La Salle, in honor of his French King Louis XIV. In 1803, France sold Louisiana to the United States as part of the Louisiana _____.
2. Spanish _____ hangs from live oak, bald cypress, and other trees. The plant has no roots and absorbs its moisture from the air. In the past, the moss was used for padding, packing, and even furniture stuffing. Since the invention of synthetic fibers, Cajun moss pickers are rare today.
4. Edward Avery McIlhenny waded through swamps to collect young snowy _____ birds that were in danger of becoming extinct because of hunting. The birds are now protected and can be seen at Avery Island Jungle Gardens. This is not a real island, but, instead, a salt dome. The McIlhennys also developed Tabasco, a hot pepper sauce.
5. John _____ Audubon was a conservationist and artist. He painted at least 75 of his famous bird paintings at Oakley Plantation House (1821-25). He eventually created 435 paintings of over 1,000 birds. His *Birds of America* is considered to be one of the greatest collections of prints ever produced.
7. Some of the settlers of Louisiana were called _____. They are descended from French settlers who left the Acadia region of Eastern Canada (Nova Scotia).
9. Mardi _____, or "Fat Tuesday," is a big Louisiana party that occurs each year 47 days before Easter. There are parades with floats, feasts, and carnival balls. People wear colorful masks and costumes.

Chickadee

Pine Tree State

White pine cone and tassel

Fill in the answers to the following questions. A few clues are given.

1. Maine is an important fishing area for herring, cod, ocean perch, scallops, shrimp, haddock, and clams but especially for this saltwater crustacean that is a popular delicacy. _ _ _ _ _ E O

2. This small peninsula near Lubec is the easternmost point in the United States, where the sun first shines on the country each day. _ O _ _ _ O _ _ A _

3. He was the most well-known U.S. poet in the 1800s. He was born in Portland. Some of his famous poems include *Evangeline, Paul Revere's Ride,* and *The Song of Hiawatha*. _ _ O _ O _ L _ _ _

4. This Wilderness Waterway is 98 miles of rivers and lakes that is one of the great areas for canoe trips in the country. _ _ L O _ O _

5. In 1775, this British ship surrendered to patriots from Machias who rowed out into the harbor, attacked the ship, and shot the captain. This battle was the first naval battle of the Revolutionary War. _ _ E _ _ _ _ O _ _ _ _

6. This is the only national park in the Northeast United States. This place of woodlands, lakes, seashores, and mountains lies on Isle au Haut and Mount Desert Island. _ O _ _ I _ _

7. This county is so large that the states of Rhode Island and Connecticut would both fit into the area. More potatoes are grown here than in any other U.S. county. The children are excused from school each fall to help harvest. _ R _ _ _ _ O _

8. This Wildlife Refuge was named for the nature writer from Kennebunkport who warned of environmental dangers. The refuge protects animals, including moose. _ _ _ O _ L _ _ _ _ _ O

9. This writer from Brunswick wrote *Uncle Tom's Cabin,* which told of the terrible living conditions and treatment of slaves. The book helped cause the Civil War. O _ _ _ E

10. Maine is known for its beautiful Atlantic coastline with beaches, harbors, fishing villages, and islands. These buildings were built to warn clipper ships and whalers away from the dangerous rocks. _ O _ _ _ _ _ U _ _ _

Write the letters found in the circles. Unscramble these letters until they provide the answer to the name of the people whose ancestors were pushed out of French Canada by the British in 1775. Even today, they maintain much of their French heritage in northern Maine.

_ _ _ _ _ _   _ _ _ _ _ _ _

© Instructional Fair • TS Denison   19   IF2736 50 States

Baltimore oriole

Old Line State

Black-eyed Susan

Locate the answers to the following questions in the word search.

1. _____ Bay, which almost divides Maryland in half, is the largest bay in the United States. With its many inlets, it is a popular vacation spot and important fishing center for soft-shell crabs, oysters, clams, and fish.
2. Maryland was the first colony officially to practice _____ tolerance, where all faiths were welcome, not just the Catholics who founded the colony in 1649.
3. "The Star-Spangled Banner" was written by Francis Scott Key as a poem (later put to music) during the War of 1812 when he could not believe the American flag was still flying over Fort _____ at Baltimore, after being bombarded all night by the British fleet.
4. Breeders developed the only pure strain of dogs created in the United States, the Chesapeake Bay _____, with ancestors being the Newfoundland, otter hound, and setters.
5. Camp _____, named for President Eisenhower's grandson, has been a retreat center, a place to rest and think, for over 50 years for U.S. presidents.
6. Annapolis is known for its many colonial buildings, is the state capital, and is the site of the U.S. _____ Academy, where men and women are trained as officers for the navy and marines.
7. Maryland is called the "Old _____ State" because its "troops of the line" Revolutionary War soldiers fought with special valor in the Battle of Long Island in 1776 and earned praise from General George Washington.
8. _____ Herman "Babe" Ruth, born in Baltimore, was a popular baseball player who became famous as a batter when he hit 714 home runs during his career, a record that was not beaten until 1974 by Hank Aaron.
9. _____ is Maryland's official state sport. Riders on horseback, carrying poles called lances, try to spear dangling rings. This is somewhat different from the sport of the Middle Ages in Europe, in which knights tried to knock one another off their horses with lances.
10. _____ Tubman and Frederick Douglass were both born in Maryland as slaves but escaped and helped fight slavery. Tubman was called "The Moses of Her People" because she helped over 300 slaves escape the plantations along the Underground Railroad, not a real rail track but instead a name for an escape route. Douglass spoke and wrote against slavery and began the *North Star*, an anti-slavery newspaper.

```
C O P Y F I S H D C R A B U
F H O X R E L I G I O U S M
R S E T O N S A L A V A N B
E E S A V G E O R G E A O R
D T E I R R A H T U N A D E
C C D N O T G N C K I N G L
R J O U S T I N G M L E F L
I O I L R E V E I R T E R A
E K A E P A S E H C S A W S
K N A T L A Q U A R I U M H
```

© Instructional Fair • TS Denison   20   IF2736 50 States

★ Massachusetts ★

Chickadee   **Bay State**   Mayflower

Locate the answers to the following questions in the word search.

1. Hunting whales for their oil made _____ a great port until another type of oil (petroleum) was discovered in Pennsylvania in 1857. (two words)
2. Many famous authors have lived in Massachusetts, including Dickinson, Emerson, Thoreau, Wheatley, Hawthorne, Poe, and more recently, Dr. _____, who wrote famous children's books, including *The Cat in the Hat*.
3. James _____ invented basketball in 1891 in Springfield, using peach baskets and a soccer ball. It was a game that could be played indoors in the winter.
4. America's oldest city park is Boston _____, which, over the years, has been where Benjamin Franklin grazed his cows, soldiers practiced drills, people who broke laws were dunked in Frog Pond, and today is the site of swan boats and a lovely place to relax in downtown Boston.
5. The Pilgrims arrived aboard the *Mayflower* from England in 1620 in search of religious freedom, created the first self-government in America with the *Mayflower* _____, and became well-known for their first Thanksgiving celebration with the Native Americans.
6. The Massachusetts Bay Colony _____, who also came from England in search of religious freedom, founded Salem and Boston, started America's first public school, and built Harvard, America's first college.
7. This hook-shaped peninsula, _____, and the nearby islands, are popular vacation areas with beaches, clam digging, surf casting, and historic, quaint towns. (two words)
8. In the 1600s, many people believed in witches who could cause bad weather and even make people die, so during 1692 and 1693, hundreds of people in the _____ area accused others of being witches, and 20 people were put to death.
9. Massachusetts leads the nation in the growing of _____, producing about 200 million pounds each year, in bogs (shallow marshes) that farmers flood each winter to protect the crops from frost.
10. Massachusetts led the fight against England in the Revolutionary War with the Boston Massacre, Boston Tea Party, the ride of Paul Revere, and the battles of Lexington and _____.

```
F E L A H W C M C T E A
C H P A R K O E L E X I
N O T S O B M L E M A J
T W D O C E P A C G O D
N I N D R S A S I S T E
A E R O A T C A N C G B
I O W I N O T A B A D R
S A A B B U T T E R R N
M W A R E I H S I F O Y
I N T O R D A I R M C N
T R W U R E F R M I N O
H O P N I C E O T W O L
B A L D E J C A R U C O
S S U E S W O N S D E C
```

© Instructional Fair • TS Denison   21   IF2736 50 States

Robin — Wolverine State — Apple blossom

Place the answers to the questions in the crossword puzzle.

Across

3. Michigan has many farms which produce cherries, cucumbers for pickles, blueberries, apples, Christmas trees, and more. In 1904, Joseph Cannon, Speaker of the House of Representatives, put through a bill in Congress to serve navy bean soup every day in the U.S. _____ dining room. This was to honor Michigan's large bean crop. The soup is famous.
5. Michigan is the only state divided into two _____, Upper and Lower. In 1957, the 5-mile long Mackinac Bridge, known as "Big Mac," was opened to connect them. The Upper is less populated and quite rural. The Lower has the largest cities and most of the agriculture and industry.
8. Sleeping Bear _____ National Seashore is one of the world's biggest sand piles. Glaciers pushed rock, sand, and silt from the north to create the huge dunes, some nearly 500' tall. The dunes look like a bear taking a nap.
10. Henry Ford was famous for his development of the _____. He built his first Ford in 1896. He is known for building his cars on an assembly line for efficiency. Other early Michigan carmakers included Ransom Olds, David Buick, and John and Horace Dodge. Michigan was a good state for car manufacturing because iron ore, which was made into iron and steel for cars, was mined here.

Down

1. Isle Royale is the state's only national park. It is a densely forested island that has a large herd of _____. The island also has wolves.
2. The town of Battle Creek is the world's largest producer of _____ cereal. John and William Kellogg were interested in health foods. John was a physician. The brothers created corn and wheat flakes, a new kind of cereal. Charles Post was a patient of Dr. Kellogg's. He was also interested in health foods and invented Grape Nuts. Around 1900, Charles Post and William Kellogg formed cereal companies.
4. No cars are allowed on Mackinac _____, but tourists enjoy walking, hiking, biking, and riding in horse-drawn carriages around this scenic resort island. Fort Mackinac was built on the island by the British in 1780. It is now a living-history museum.
6. Lake Huron is 26' lower than its neighbor, Lake Superior, so a canal called the Soo Canal and Locks was built at _____ Sainte Marie. Soo Locks connects the two lakes by raising and lowering the water level so ships can go from one lake to the other.
7. The town of Holland was founded in 1840 by Dutch people. The town has an old _____ from The Netherlands. Each spring, the town hosts a famous Tulip Festival. The people dress in traditional clothes and dance in wooden shoes.
9. Some of the members of the U.S. 10th Mountain Brigade fought on skis to control the Italian Alps during World ___ II. They returned to their native state of Michigan and helped start ski resorts.

© Instructional Fair • TS Denison — IF2736 50 States

Common loon

★ MINNESOTA ★
Gopher State

Pink-and-white lady's slipper

Fill in the lines with the answers to the questions. Then arrange the answers to fit into the puzzle boxes.

_____ 1. Minnesota leads the nation in the mining of this mineral, found mainly in the Mesabi, Vermillion, and Cuyana ranges (two words).

_____ 2. At Grand Portage National Monument, costumed guides dress like these Frenchmen who came in canoes to bring tools and clothes for North West Company traders to exchange for beaver and other furs.

_____ 3. Indians carved peace pipes from this soft red stone, found only at this site that is considered sacred ground and now is a national monument.

_____ 4. This lake is the source of the Mississippi River.

_____ 5. Boundary Waters is the nation's only wilderness preserved for people who travel in this type of boat.

_____ 6. During the last ice age, much of Minnesota was buried under these, and they scoured the land underneath. This movement uncovered valuable iron ore deposits, dumped fertile soils in parts of the state, and created over 15,000 lakes.

_____ 7. The Chippewa Indians harvested this crop by guiding their canoes through marshes, pulling the head of this grain over the canoe, and shaking the ripe grain loose (two words).

_____ 8. This rock with ancient writing on it may have been left by Norsemen who may have come to Minnesota over 100 years before Columbus left Spain.

_____ 9. More of this type of moss, used by gardeners to improve soils, is found in Minnesota bogs than in any other state.

_____ 10. Charles Schulz was born in Minneapolis. He created this comic strip that appears in over 2,000 newspapers in many countries.

© Instructional Fair • TS Denison   23   IF2736 50 States

Mockingbird   **Magnolia State**   Magnolia

Fill in the answers to the following questions. A few clues are given.

1. In 1954, the U.S. Supreme Court said racial segregation in schools was unlawful, but Mississippi did not change. Accompanied by federal troops in 1962, this man was the first black to enroll at the University of Mississippi.   _ (_) M _ _ _   _ _ _ _ _ (_) _ _

2. These beautiful pre-Civil War houses belonged to cotton plantation owners and are well preserved today for visitors, especially in Natchez.   A _ _ _ _ (_) _ _ _ _ _ _
_ _ (_) _ _ _

3. This was a crucial Civil War battle. The North captured this town, giving it control of the Mississippi River.   _ _ _ _ (_) S _ (_) _ _

4. This city is a beautiful Gulfcoast resort that attracts visitors to the world's longest artificially created beach. The city has an important shrimp industry, too.   _ _ I (_) _ _ _

5. He was born in Greenville and is known for creating Kermit the Frog, Miss Piggy, and other Sesame Street Muppets.   _ _ _   _ (_) N _ _ _

6. These were Mississippi River boats that put on musicals, dramas, and other entertainment. A famous one was the Floating Circus Palace, which seated over 3,000 people.   _ _ _ (_) _ _ A _ _ _

7. These fish are grown commercially in ponds called "farms" where they are cared for like livestock. Farmers can grow as much as 5,000 pounds of high-protein meat per acre.   _ _ T (_) _ _ _

8. The sacred mounds of these native people are preserved at Emerald Mound and at Nanih Waiya Historic Site.   _ _ _ _ T (_) _

9. This important road was built from Nashville, Tennessee, to Natchez. It was especially used by boatmen who traveled down the Mississippi River but found it easier to return by land and not fight the river's strong current.   (_) _ _ C _ _ _   _ (_) _ _

10. The first time this holiday was celebrated was after the Civil War in 1866, when several ladies from Columbus decorated the graves of Confederate and Union soldiers at Friendship Cemetery.   (_) _ _ _   R _ (_)   _ _ _

Write the letters found in the circles. Unscramble these letters until they provide the answer to the name of this Nobel Prize and Pulitzer Prize author from Oxford. This author wrote many novels about the history and families of an imaginary Mississippi county, Yoknapatawpha.

_ _ _ _ _ _   _ _ _ _ _ _ _ _ _

© Instructional Fair • TS Denison   24   IF2736 50 States

Bluebird

 ★ MISSOURI ★

Show Me State

Hawthorn flower

Write the letter from Column B that most correctly answers the description found in Column A. Note: More choices are given in Column B than will be used for answers.

Column A

_____ 1. Author and humorist who was raised in Hannibal and wrote stories about Tom Sawyer and Huckleberry Finn, telling tales of his own childhood.

_____ 2. Stands for "intelligent skepticism" and was first said by Congressman Willard Vandiver in 1899, in response to another Congressman's boasting about his state.

_____ 3. Relays of expert horse riders who carried the mail in 1860-1861 across the country, starting in St. Joseph.

_____ 4. Rugged hills that attract visitors to the many caves, forests, and lakes, including Lake of the Ozarks.

_____ 5. Famous Missouri plant scientist who taught farmers to plant peanuts, sweet potatoes, and soybeans.

_____ 6. Missouri is the #1 state for the mining of this metal.

_____ 7. America's tallest monument, built along the St. Louis waterfront, with a 630' high stainless steel arch known as the "Gateway to the West." It contains a museum telling about explorers, fur trappers, and pioneers.

_____ 8. Hot dogs, ice cream cones, and iced tea were first sold at the 1904 World's Fair held in this city.

_____ 9. Missouri has about 5,000 of these, more than any other state, including Meramec, with one room large enough to hold 300 cars.

_____ 10. He attended art school in Kansas City. He created famous cartoon characters and theme parks. His Mainstreet, USA, is based on his hometown, Marceline.

Column B

A. Missouri Compromise of 1820
B. St. Louis
C. Jefferson National Expansion Memorial
D. "Mother of the West"
E. Caves
F. "Show me"
G. Walt Disney
H. Santa Fe Trail
I. Dred Scott Decision
J. Samuel Clemens
K. Ozark Plateau
L. Canyons
M. Lead
N. George Washington Carver
O. Hallmark Cards
P. President Harry S Truman
Q. Pony Express

© Instructional Fair • TS Denison   25   IF2736 50 States

Western meadowlark

Treasure State

Bitterroot

Write the letter from Column B that most correctly answers the description found in Column A. Note: More choices are given in Column B than will be used for answers.

Column A

_____ 1. One of the nation's last big herds of bison lives here, now surviving well after nearly being hunted to extinction.

_____ 2. This town calls itself "the richest hill on earth" because of the mining of gold, silver, and especially copper.

_____ 3. He and other Nez Perce Indians were captured by U.S. soldiers in 1877 in northern Montana, just before they reached safety and sanctuary in Canada

_____ 4. At the Battle of the Little Bighorn, he and other men of the U.S. Cavalry were killed by Sioux and Cheyenne Indians who were fighting to save their way of life.

_____ 5. National park known for beautiful lakes, waterfalls, wildlife, and mountains with over 50 glaciers

_____ 6. Explorers who struggled over a month to get around the Great Falls of the Missouri and who found the source of the Missouri River

_____ 7. Prospectors came to Montana for this metal, hearing it was so plentiful that one could yank up a sagebrush, shake off the sand from its roots, and pan about a dollar's worth!

_____ 8. This Montana dinosaur means "good mother reptile." Skeletons of the adult were found with nests and babies.

_____ 9. The Continental Divide usually divides east- and west-flowing water, but from this pass, waters eventually flow into the Atlantic, Pacific, and Hudson Bay.

_____ 10. He was not only the sheriff of Bannack and Virginia City, but also secretly headed a gang that robbed stagecoaches. He was caught and hanged.

Column B

A. Henry Plummer
B. Crazy Horse
C. Grace Eldering
D. George A. Custer
E. Glacier
F. National Bison Range
G. Bozeman
H. Maiasaura
I. Pompey's Pillar
J. Lewis and Clark
K. Butte
L. Triple Divide Pass
M. Chief Joseph
N. Bighorn Canyon
O. Tyrannosaurus rex
P. Charles M. Russell
Q. Gold
R. Yellowstone National Park

© Instructional Fair • TS Denison   26   IF2736 50 States

Western meadowlark • **Corn Husker State** • Goldenrod

Locate the answers to the following questions in the word search.

1. Daniel Freeman's home near Beatrice is now _____ National Monument. The monument honors him as the first person to take advantage of the Homestead Act of 1862, which gave 160 acres of land to each settler.
2. There often were not enough trees for the homes of settlers. Instead, they borrowed a trick from the Indians. They built out of "Nebraska marble," which was tough prairie _____ cut into building blocks for their homes.
3. Nebraska's nickname is based on the University of Nebraska Cornhuskers, since _____ is so popular. It is said that on Saturdays when there is a home game, the stadium becomes "the third largest city in the state."
4. J. Sterling North of Nebraska City started _____ because the state had so few trees, and he wanted to convince others to plant trees. It is now celebrated across the country. (two words)
5. "Buffalo" Bill Cody staged the "Old Glory Blowout," which was a famous rodeo in North Platte. In 1883, he organized Buffalo Bill's _____ Show, which toured the United States and Europe. (two words)
6. _____ Fossil Beds National Monument contains the fossil remains of mammals that lived in the region about 22 million years ago. Visitors can see bones of extinct animals that might have been ancestors of the modern rhinoceros, horse, pig, deer, and other mammals.
7. The SAC (_____ Air Command) at Offutt Air Force Base is one of America's most important defense systems. It provides bomber and missile protection. Visitors can see a five-screen reenactment of a SAC "red alert," as well as a display of many planes and guided missiles.
8. There are unusual rock formations that look like monsters and dinosaurs at _____ National Grasslands near Crawford. Toadstool Park is a section of the grasslands where many prehistoric animal fossils have been found.
9. Father Edward Flanagan, a Catholic priest, said, "There's no such thing as a bad boy" when he founded _____ in 1917. Girls are now also welcome at this home and school for neglected, abandoned, or underprivileged children. (two words)
10. The most famous writer to be associated with Nebraska is Willa _____. *O Pioneers!* was published in 1913, the first of many books about pioneer life on the Nebraska frontier. Her novel *One of Ours*, about a Nebraska farmer who died in World War I, won the 1923 Pulitzer Prize for fiction.

```
O Y S T U H R C M G S
M E A P O N Y I K E C
A S E D E T A G A R O
H T R A R N I E C L T
A S H E D O S T L L T
R E H T A C B A L D S
W W A S U E B R U F B
H D I E S T E T A O L
E L I M O I L S I R U
A I B O Y S T O W N F
T W F H A L A L G O F
C H I M N E Y R O C K
```

© Instructional Fair • TS Denison   27   IF2736 50 States

Mountain bluebird **Silver State** **Sagebrush**

Fill in the lines with the answers to the questions. Then, arrange the answers to fit into the puzzle boxes.

_____ 1. Historic mining town that grew up along the Comstock Lode and today is popular with tourists who visit the restored mansions, mines, churches, and saloons. (two words)

_____ 2. One of the richest deposits of silver in world history; it helped the North pay its Civil War expenses. (two words)

_____ 3. Largest city in Nevada and one of the few cities in the United States where gambling is legal. The city is also known worldwide for its neon lights, casinos, hotels with theme parks, and entertainment. (two words)

_____ 4. Massive dam that holds back the mighty Colorado River, creating Lake Mead.

_____ 5. This beautiful lake, surrounded by snow-capped mountains, is one of the deepest lakes in the country.

_____ 6. Chief of northern Paiutes who worked hard to maintain peace with white settlers and signed the treaty with the whites to end the Pyramid Lake War.

_____ 7. National park that has miles of hiking trails, alpine lakes and meadows, Lehman Caves, Wheeler Peak, and one of the world's largest groves of ancient bristlecone pine trees. (two words)

_____ 8. For years, this Norwegian, nicknamed "Snowshoe," carried the mail through the Sierra Nevada Mountains from California to Genoa, Nevada, and introduced the use of skis to the United States.

_____ 9. He was called "The Pathfinder," because he explored and mapped the Great Basin and Sierra Nevada regions during a U.S. government-sponsored scientific expedition, which some believe was a spy mission.

_____ 10. In 1861, these were imported from Asia and put to work hauling salt from a dry marsh near Comstock. Although they survived in the desert, they scared the horses, and their use was soon abandoned.

© Instructional Fair • TS Denison 28 IF2736 50 States

 # New Hampshire

Purple finch   **Granite State**   Purple lilac

Locate the answers to the following questions in the word search.

1. Sarah _____, born in Newport, was a writer and editor who wrote the well-known children's poem, "Mary Had a Little Lamb." She also worked to have Thanksgiving made into a national holiday.
2. The Mt. Washington _____ Railway was the first one of its kind built in the United States, and on a clear day, from the top of the mountain, tourists have a scenic view of four states, Canada, and the Atlantic Ocean.
3. The _____ Mountains got their name from being made of granite, a very hard rock that looks white in the sunlight.
4. New Hampshire has had two famous astronauts, Alan _____, the first American astronaut in space (1961), and Christa McAuliffe, the teacher-in-space who died tragically in the space shuttle *Challenger* explosion in 1986.
5. Chinook sled dogs, bred in New Hampshire, went on _____ Byrd's Antarctic exploration and worked with the army's search-and-rescue units. Today, the World Champion Sled Dog Derby occurs each winter on Lake Winnipesaukee.
6. The world record for the highest wind _____ was 231 mph, which is even stronger than hurricane winds. This was recorded in 1934 atop Mt. Washington.
7. At _____ Village, started in 1792 in Canterbury, visitors can see historic buildings and crafts from this religious group that got its name from shaking while dancing during worship.
8. At Franconia Notch, a famous natural rock formation looks like the profile of a human face and is called The Old Man of the _____.
9. In the 1800s, Amoskeag Mills became the biggest _____ plant in the world. It produced 147,000 miles of cloth each year, but is now closed.
10. Every four years, New Hampshire's presidential _____ election, where people vote on the final candidates to run for president, makes the news as the first election held in the country. This is a tradition from years ago, when people voted in February before the spring thaw turned the roads to mud and made travel difficult.

```
P I R O N N O D R A P E H S
O N C E P W I N D I M F H A
R D O O R I N A D M I R A L
T E X T I L E I T I L O L D
S P A V M L A M B N L S E A
D E T I A E W A L K U T A R
R N S L R F H O G H T O O T
O D I L Y T I C O L E V M N
C E R A E E T E C A P S A O
N N H G S R E K A H S O Y U
O C C E D O G B R I D G E T
C E C O V E R E D N O T C H
```

© Instructional Fair • TS Denison   IF2736 50 States

Eastern goldfinch — Garden State — Purple violet

Fill in the answers to the following questions. A few clues are given.

1. She became a well-known Civil War nurse and then became the first American Red Cross President in 1880.
   _ _ _ _ _ _ _ R _ Ⓞ

2. Resort city with a wooden walkway called the Boardwalk, a beach, casinos, arcades, amusement parks, shops, restaurants, hotels, and the annual Miss America Pageant.
   _ _ _ _ A _ _ _ _ _ Ⓞ _ _

3. At Haddonfield in 1858, a scientist identified the fossilized skeleton of this first dinosaur discovered in North America.
   Ⓞ _ _ _ _ _ _ _ _ _ _

4. In 1846, Hoboken was the site of the first game of this pro sport.
   Ⓞ _ _ _ _ _ L _

5. He invented over 1,000 items, including the phonograph, electric light bulb, and motion picture camera, in his lab at Menlo Park.
   _ H _ _ _ _ Ⓞ _ _ _

6. The Pine Barrens is a swampy part of the state where oaks, cedars, and dwarf pines grow. Many people work in the "bogs," raising this fruit.
   _ Ⓞ _ _ _ _ _ _ _ _ S

7. This provides employment for people in cities because factories make many products including chemicals, paints, medicine, and soap.
   M _ _ Ⓞ _ _ _ _ _ _ _ _ _

8. Although it is the most densely populated state, much of New Jersey is used as this because of the fertile soil where flowers and food are grown.
   F _ _ _ _ _ _ Ⓞ

9. Atlantic City, with streets named Boardwalk, Atlantic Avenue, Marvin Gardens, and Park Place, was the inspiration for Charles Darrow to invent this board game during the Great Depression in 1930.
   _ _ Ⓞ _ _ L _

10. This National Wildlife Refuge is near the urban area of New Jersey close to New York City. It is a valuable wilderness area, filled with many animals, but is threatened by pollution and urban growth.
    Ⓞ _ _ _ _ _ W _ _ _

Write the letters found in the circles. Unscramble these letters to find the name of the famous German airship, filled with hydrogen gas to keep it aloft, that exploded at Lakehurst in 1937. It killed 36 people and ended the age of the airship for passenger service.

_ _ _ _ _ _ _ _ _

© Instructional Fair • TS Denison
IF2736 50 States

Roadrunner

 # New Mexico
Land of Enchantment

Yucca

Write the letter from Column B that most correctly answers the description found in Column A. Note: More choices are given in Column B than will be used for answers.

Column A

_____ 1. Magnificent chambers formed during earth's upheaval and the seeping of minerals and water through limestone

_____ 2. Near Alamogordo in 1945, the first was exploded, creating a fireball so hot it turned the desert sand to glass.

_____ 3. Site of the world's largest gypsum desert, with high, white shifting dunes

_____ 4. This large radio telescope near Socorro is an instrument astronomers use to collect radio sound waves from space, some billions of years old, to learn about the history of the universe.

_____ 5. Founded by the Spanish in 1709-1710, today it is the oldest seat of government in the United States.

_____ 6. First European road in the United States, running from Santa Fe to Chihuahua, Mexico, opened in 1581 by the Spanish.

_____ 7. Well-known frontiersman, trapper, guide, and explorer, who settled down in Taos as the Indian agent for the Apache and Ute Indians

_____ 8. Rescued after a 1950 forest fire near Capitan, he became a symbol for outdoor fire safety and lived at the National Zoo in Washington, D.C.

_____ 9. Around A.D. 1000, this was the center of the most sophisticated society north of Mexico and was home to 13 "cities," with Pueblo Bonito being the most impressive.

_____ 10. Route traders and emigrants traveled from Missouri to Santa Fe between 1821-1880

Column B

A. El Camino Real
B. Albuquerque
C. Smokey Bear
D. Georgia O'Keefe
E. Santa Fe Trail
F. Carlsbad Caverns National Park
G. Christopher "Kit" Carson
H. Adobe
I. Very Large Array (VLA)
J. Los Alamos National Laboratory
K. Chaco Culture National Historical Park
L. Coelophysis
M. White Sands National Monument
N. Sandia man
O. Atomic bomb
P. Stephen Kearny
Q. Santa Fe
R. Uranium
S. Sangre de Cristos
T. Bandelier National Monument

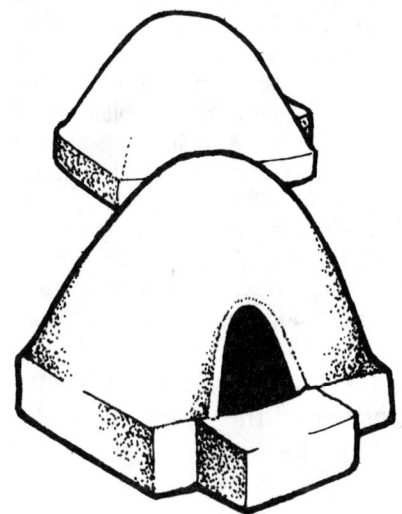

© Instructional Fair • TS Denison IF2736 50 States

Bluebird   **Empire State**   Rose

Fill in the answers to the following questions. A few clues are given.

1. She organized the country's first Women's Rights Convention, held in Seneca Falls. The participants felt women should have the right to vote. _ _ _ _ _ _ T _ _ _Ⓐ_ _ _

2. American Falls and Horseshoe Falls make up this great natural wonder of thundering water. Daredevils have illegally tumbled over the falls in barrels. _Ⓞ_ _ _ _ _ _ _ _ L _

3. This city is called the "Big Apple" and is known for Central Park, World Trade Center, Wall Street, Coney Island, Bronx Zoo, Broadway, Times Square, museums, and more. _ _ _ _ _ R _ Ⓞ _ _

4. New York City was settled by this nationality of people. In 1625, Governor Peter Minuit bought Manhattan Island from the local Indians for $24 worth of trinkets. Ⓞ_ _ _ C _

5. This is an extensive system of canals, rivers, and lakes that connect the Atlantic Ocean with the Great Lakes. It forms the border of Canada and the United States. _ _ . _ _ _ W _ _Ⓞ_ _   _ _ _ _ _ _

6. This thirty-second president of the United States lived in Hyde Park. He helped the country through the Depression with his New Deal program that changed the banking system and financed public projects. _ _ _ _ _ _ L _ _ Ⓞ _ _ _ _ _ _ _ _ _

7. This waterway ran from Albany on the Hudson River to Buffalo on the shores of Lake Erie. Barges were towed by horses or mules that walked over a towpath next to the canal. _Ⓞ_ _ E _ _ _ _ _

8. This is the site of the National Baseball Hall of Fame where the great players of the game are honored. _ _Ⓞ_ _ _ S _ _ _ _

9. This man was born poor in Richford but ended up a millionaire. He established Standard Oil. During his lifetime, he gave $550 million to schools, charities, and foundations. _ _ _ _ _ _ . _ _ _Ⓞ_ E _ _ _ _

10. This was a gift to the United States from France in 1886. It stands on Liberty Island in New York Harbor. It was the first landmark sighted by immigrants coming by ship to start a new life of freedom in the United States. _ _Ⓞ_ _ _ _   _ I _ _ _ _ _

Write the letters found in the circles. Unscramble these letters until they provide the answer to the name of this mountain range which includes forested land, over 200 lakes, and about 100 mountains, including Mt. Marcy.

_ _ _ _ _ _ _ _ _ _

© Instructional Fair • TS Denison   32   IF2736 50 States

North Carolina

Cardinal

Tar Heel State

Flowering dogwood

Place the answers to the questions in the crossword puzzle:

Across
1. Kill _____ Hill near Kitty Hawk was the site of the Wright Brothers' first self-powered airplane flight in 1903. This site on the Outer Banks was chosen for its winds and soft sand. The plane stayed up for 12 seconds and flew 120'.
4. This state's people have the nickname Tar _____. There are several stories of how this name originated. One story says it started during the Revolutionary War when colonial patriots dumped tar from pine trees into a stream, hoping to stop the British from crossing. The colonists succeeded. Another story says that during the Civil War, the soldiers from North Carolina stuck fiercely to their positions as if they were held by tar.
8. North Carolina was the first state to instruct its delegates to the Continental Congress to vote for _____ from England. That date, April 12, 1776, appears on the state's flag.
10. In 1585, the first English colony was established at _____ Island. The people had many problems and returned to England. In 1587, a second colony was started. Governor White returned to England for supplies. When he returned in 1590, all of the settlers were gone. He was unable to search for them. Today it is known as the "Lost Colony."

Down
2. Some potatoes native to North Carolina were taken to _____ from Roanoke Island. They became that country's major food crop.
3. Cape _____ is known as the "Graveyard of the Atlantic" because of its shallow sands. This is a popular seashore area. The Outer Banks have wild ponies which may be descendants of horses brought by the Spanish hundreds of years ago.
5. North Carolina has many beautiful mountains. The Blue Ridge Parkway is a road that follows the crest of the mountains past scenic viewpoints. One of these is Grandfather Mountain. The peak looks like the face of a sleeping old man. North Carolina shares the Great Smoky Mountains National Park with _____.
6. The town of _____ is home to descendants of the Indians who hid in the hills in the 1830s and escaped the troops that drove Southeastern Indians along the "Trail of Tears" to be resettled in Oklahoma. In this town is Oconaluftee, a recreated Indian village of the 1700s.
7. North Carolina is known for three major manufactured goods—tobacco products, wooden furniture, and _____ (cloth goods). For example, Greensboro has the world's largest mill for weaving denim.
9. Virginia _____ was born in Roanoke Colony in 1587. She was the first English baby born in America. She was named Virginia because, at that time, the colony was called Virginia.

© Instructional Fair • TS Denison

IF2736 50 States

NORTH DAKOTA

Western meadowlark

Flickertail State

Wild prairie rose

Fill in the lines with the answers to the questions. Then arrange the answers to fit into the puzzle boxes.

_____ 1. This future president loved his two North Dakota cattle ranches. Later, they became the only national park created in the memory of a single person.

_____ 2. This area of strange land formations, created from years of wind and water erosion, got this name because early travelers found the region difficult to cross.

_____ 3. After Lewis and Clark spent the winter of 1804 at Fort Mandan, they added this Shoshone Indian woman to their expedition as an interpreter.

_____ 4. More of this type of bird migrates to North Dakota each summer to breed and to feed in the lakes, marshes, and grain fields than in any other state.

_____ 5. Years ago, this type of underground coal caught fire from a campfire or lightning and is still burning.

_____ 6. Another nickname for North Dakota refers to this type of garden which celebrates the many years of friendship between the United States and Canada.

_____ 7. This is the Sioux Indian word meaning "allies" or "friends," also called Lakota.

_____ 8. This valley is a fertile and beautiful agricultural region of North Dakota that cowboys used to sing about. (two words)

_____ 9. Since North and South Dakota were signed into statehood on the same day in 1889, this president covered the names as he signed the papers so neither state could brag about being first.

_____ 10. This 15-year-old girl became a hero when she was walking home from school with her younger brother and sister. During a blizzard when the horse-drawn sled overturned, she lay on top of them to save their lives, but she froze to death. (two words)

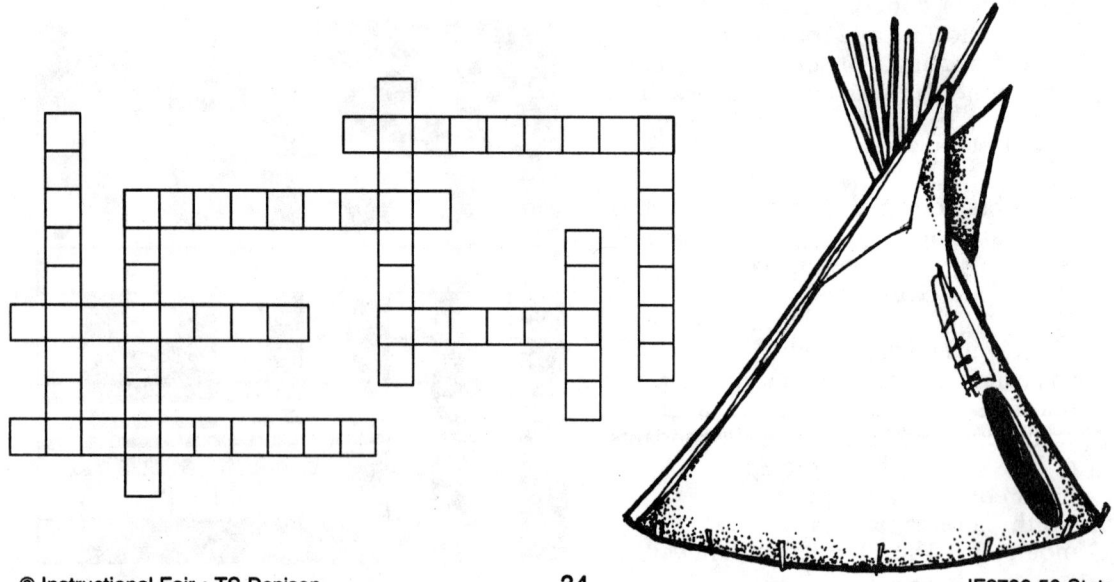

© Instructional Fair • TS Denison   34   IF2736 50 States

★ Ohio ★

Cardinal

Buckeye State

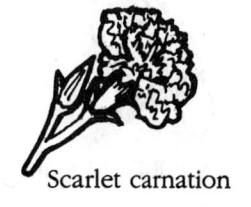

Scarlet carnation

Locate the answers to the following questions in the word search.

1. In 1951, a _____ radio announcer, Alan Freed, named a new kind of music which is now honored at the Rock and Roll Hall of Fame.
2. The state is named for the buckeye, a form of horse chestnut tree, whose nut looks like the eye of a _____ when opened.
3. _____ College was the first higher education institution in the United States to enroll both men and women and one of the first colleges to enroll blacks.
4. Since the National Football League was started in _____, it is the site of the Pro Football Hall of Fame, a museum dedicated to the history and to the best players of the game.
5. About 3,000 years ago, Indians of the Midwest began building burial and ceremonial mounds, some in very unusual shapes, such as _____ Mound near Hillsboro.
6. Ohio is a leading manufacturing state. It is known for its tall smokestacks of power plants, factories, and steel mills. It has been working to clean up its pollution, especially after the incident in 1969 when the oil-slicked water of the _____ River actually caught fire.
7. Ohio is the home of two famous astronauts, John _____, the first American to orbit the earth (1962), and Neil Armstrong, the first man to walk on the moon (1969).
8. Harvey Firestone of Akron found a way to make safe, inflatable tires, so Akron became a world leader in _____ manufacturing, especially as the headquarters of many tire-making plants. Akron is now also known for its plastics production and the annual All-American Soap Box Derby.
9. Ohio is known as the "Mother of Presidents" because seven of them were born in Ohio: Ulysses Grant, William McKinley, William Taft, James Garfield, Rutherford Hayes, William H. Harrison, and Benjamin _____.
10. Starting in 1801, John Chapman believed he had a holy mission to plant fruit trees for pioneer families, so he got apple seeds from cider presses and planted about 1,200 acres of trees in Central Ohio. This earned him the nickname of John _____.

```
N S D A Y T O A M I S H A Y E
A P N C G C H S T E E L A K E
Y E A K N O I H A R R I S O N
B I L T U B H V A P P L E R N
R L E R E E D A I R E M O U O
E B V T I R E S Y E N A H B T
D E E S E L P P A U T P I B N
O R L O H I S T O W C S O E A
G G C H N N E L G W R I G R C
```

© Instructional Fair • TS Denison   35   IF2736 50 States

OKLAHOMA

Scissor Tailed Flycatcher

Sooner State

Mistletoe

Place the answers to the questions in the crossword puzzle:

Across
2. _____ Thorpe was born near Prague. He won two track and field gold medals at the 1929 Olympic Games in Sweden. The king of Sweden called Thorpe the "World's Greatest Athlete" after he won both the decathlon and pentathlon.
6. Oklahoma was known as the "Twin Territories." There were two parts, Indian Territory and Oklahoma Territory. The five Civilized Tribes wanted to become their own state of _____, but Congress refused. In 1907, the Oklahoma and Indian Territories united to become one state.
7. In 1897, the first profitable oil well was drilled in Bartlesville. Tulsa soon called itself the "_____ Capital of the World."
9. George Gist, known as Sequoyah, developed written symbols for each of the 86 Cherokee sounds. He spent years teaching the Cherokees to write. In 1844, the Cherokee *Advocate* was the first _____ published in Oklahoma, printed partly in English and partly in Cherokee.
10. Oklahoma suffered from a long period of dry weather in the 1930s. High winds churned up clouds of dust that ruined crops. John _____ wrote a novel, *The Grapes of Wrath*. It tells of farmers who left this Dust Bowl to get a new start in other places.

Down
1. During the winter of 1838-1839, nearly 75,000 Indians were forced to move west to Indian Territory. Their belongings were stolen or destroyed and homes were burned. This became known as the Trail of _____, because over 4,000 Indians died from cold, starvation, and disease.
3. In 1830, the U.S. Congress passed the _____ Removal Act. This allowed the government to move southeastern Indian tribes to Oklahoma. From 1830-1842, Cherokee, Creek, Seminole, Chickasaw, and Choctaw were moved to a large Indian reservation.
4. In 1889, the U.S. government bought Oklahoma Indian land for white settlement. Each family could claim 160 free acres. On April 22, thousands raced by foot, wagon, train, horseback, and even bicycle to stake their claims. About 50,000 settlers arrived that day. However, some had tried to sneak in sooner than they were supposed to, so the state became known as the _____ State. Another land rush was held Sept. 16, 1893, when over 100,000 people rushed into the Cherokee Strip.
5. Will _____, an Oklahoma native, was an entertainer, famous for his cowboy humor. He performed rope tricks while talking about politics and people. He starred in plays, movies, and on radio shows. He also wrote a newspaper column.
8. Oklahoma is known for several famous Native-American ballerinas, including Maria and Marjorie Tallchief, daughters of an Osage chief. Maria was the first American-trained ballerina to become a world star. She founded the Chicago City _____. Marjorie danced with the Paris Ballet Company.

© Instructional Fair • TS Denison

IF2736 50 States

★ OREGON ★

Meadowlark
Beaver State
Oregon grape

Fill in the lines with the answers to the questions. Then arrange the answers to fit into the puzzle boxes.

_____ 1. Deepest lake in the United States, originally called "Deep Blue Lake"

_____ 2. These "groups of trees," such as the Deschutes or the Wallowa-Whitman, cover over half of Oregon

_____ 3. Popular water sport on the Columbia River, especially at the town of Hood River

_____ 4. One of the largest rodeos in the world, held each year in northeastern Oregon

_____ 5. Mountain range that divides the rainy western side of the state from the drier eastern side

_____ 6. Fort near the Pacific Ocean where explorers Lewis and Clark spent the rainy winter of 1805-1806

_____ 7. Broad, beautiful valley that contains fertile farmlands and the state's largest cities

_____ 8. Largest city in the state, known for its roses, fountains, parks, bridges, and carousels

_____ 9. After cattle and dairy products, the leading product of the state, grown mainly in the Columbia Basin

_____ 10. "Steps" that help salmon get past Columbia River dams so they can swim back upstream to lay their eggs

© Instructional Fair • TS Denison

PENNSYLVANIA

Ruffled grouse | Keystone State | Mountain laurel

Write the letter from Column B that most correctly answers the description found in Column A. Note: More choices are given in Column B than will be used for answers.

Column A

___ 1. The hills around Pittsburgh contain bituminous coal which can be baked into coke, the fuel for blast furnaces to make this metal.

___ 2. Site of the important 1863 Civil War battle where President Lincoln, while dedicating the cemetery, issued his speech that started, "Four score and seven years ago...."

___ 3. This animal, known as Punxsutawney Phil, emerges from his hole each February 2 to tell whether spring has arrived.

___ 4. These Amish and Mennonites, actually of German and Swiss heritage, live in traditional, simple ways.

___ 5. He was awarded over 28 million acres of land, which became Pennsylvania, as a payment of a debt from King Charles II of England.

___ 6. This lady is said to have made the first American flag, at the request of George Washington.

___ 7. Over 3,000 of Washington's Revolutionary War soldiers died here during the winter of 1777-1778 from smallpox, cold, and scarce food and clothing.

___ 8. This rang from Independence Hall when the Continental Congress was in session and to proclaim the adoption of the Declaration of Independence, but it cracked in 1846.

___ 9. This Philadelphia building was the site of the signing of the Declaration of Independence and the Constitution.

___ 10. On the Susquehanna River in 1979, this was the site of the first serious nuclear accident in the United States, requiring a total shutdown of the power plant.

Column B

A. Benjamin Franklin
B. Groundhog
C. Independence Hall
D. Quakers
E. Three-Mile Island
F. Steel
G. Pocono Mountains
H. William Penn
I. Limestone
J. Gettysburg
K. Liberty Bell
L. Allegheny Plateau
M. Valley Forge
N. Pennsylvania Dutch
O. Marian Anderson
P. Little League
Q. Betsy Ross
R. Charles Conrad, Jr.

© Instructional Fair • TS Denison   IF2736 50 States

★ RHODE ISLAND ★

Rhode Island Red | Ocean State | **Violet**

Fill in the answers to the following questions. A few clues are given.

1. This describes the size of Rhode Island, just 48 by 37 miles, in relation to the other states. However, it has the longest name of any state, the State of Rhode Island and the Providence Plantations.

   _ _ (O) _ _ _ _ _ T _

2. He built America's first water-powered cotton-spinning machine in Pawtucket. His was the first factory in the United States. It started the Industrial Revolution.

   _ _ _ _ _ _ _   _ _ (O) _ E _

3. These fancy homes of wealthy merchants were built on the bluffs of Newport overlooking the ocean. Many are open today for tourists and are the site of summer music festivals.

   M _ (O) _ _ _ _ _

4. He founded Providence in 1636 as a place for religious freedom.

   _ _ (O) _ R _   _ _ _ _ _ _ (O)

5. This city leads the world in the production of costume jewelry and sterling silver products.

   _ _ _ _ _ _ _ (O) C _

6. This man from North Kingston is the artist who painted the portrait of George Washington that is found on the one-dollar bill.

   _ _ _ _ _ _ T _   _ _ _ _ (O)

7. This Ivy League university started as a college for Baptist men.

   _ (O) _ _ N

8. This lady from Newport wrote the words to "The Battle Hymn of the Republic." She also worked for women's rights and the abolition of slavery.

   _ _ _ _ I _   _ _ (O) _   _ _ _ _

9. This type of garden in Portsmouth features 80 sculptured trees and shrubs that resemble animals such as giraffes and peacocks.

   (O) _ _ _ _ _ R _

10. This type of chicken, developed in Rhode Island, was officially recognized as a new breed of poultry in 1895.

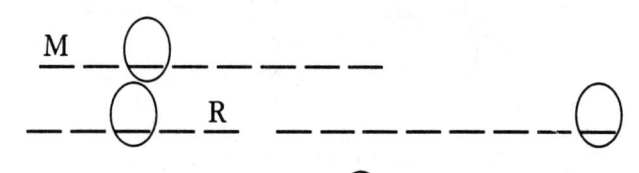

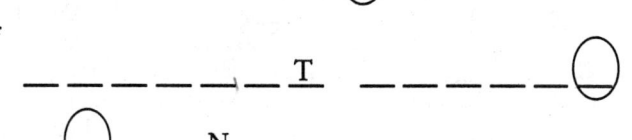

    _ _ _ _ _   _ _ _ (O) _ D _ (O) _

Write the letters found in the circles. Unscramble these letters until they provide the answer to the name of this large bay that is a popular sailboating and sport fishing center.

_ _ _ _ _ _ _ _ _ _ _

★ South Carolina ★

Carolina wren

Palmetto State

Carolina yellow jasmine

Locate the answers to the following questions in the word search.

1. Known as "King _____," this crop was the biggest in the state in the 1800s, due to the use of slave labor. Because of this crop, the textile industry began. Other farm products today include tobacco, soybeans, peaches, corn, cattle, and much more.
2. Fort _____, in Charleston Harbor, was bombed by Confederate soldiers on April 12, 1861. This act started the Civil War.
3. During the Revolutionary War in 1776, Colonel William Moulaie defended his log fort against British warships. For nine hours, the soft spongy logs of the _____ tree let the cannonballs absorb into the fort's walls, allowing the Americans to win the battle. The tree became the state's nickname.
4. South Carolina was the first state to _____ from the Union on December 20, 1860. The 11 Southern states formed the Confederate States of America.
5. Around 1835, Joel Poinsett brought the _____ flower from Mexico. It is now a popular Christmas flower in the United States.
6. South Carolina is a state known for recreation resorts along the Atlantic Ocean. There are wide sturdy beaches, water sports, tennis, golf, and biking. On a large island is the famous resort, _____ Head.
7. Mary McLeod _____ was the fifteenth of 17 children born to former slaves. Even though she was a girl and was black, she graduated from school and became a teacher. This was unusual for the late 1880s. She started a school, Bethune-Cookman College in Florida, that is known for training black teachers.
8. Founded in 1670, _____ is South Carolina's oldest city and one of the most historic in the United States. Many buildings have been carefully preserved.
9. The Venus _____ is an unusual insect-eating plant that grows in South Carolina swamps.
10. In the 1700s, pirates were a threat to South Carolina's coast. The famous pirate _____ was known for his long black beard which he tied with colored ribbons. He and his men robbed ships in Charleston Harbor. Stede Bonnet was another pirate who made people "walk the plank," jumping into the ocean to die.

```
P E A C H C O L U M B I A
B A S S O T T E M L A P S
C R E L T R U T A G C A T
L E D E C E S C P G O L F
A W H E A T K S U M T E R
Y O C R A B S H I L T O N
A I T T E S N I O P O N G
S C H A R L E S T O N T O
E W R E N P A R T Y L F H
A D E B E T H U N E F O X
```

© Instructional Fair • TS Denison   40   IF2736 50 States

South Dakota

Ring-necked pheasant

Sunshine State

American pasqueflower

Place the answers to the questions in the crossword puzzle.

Across

4. __. _____ near Rapid City is a memorial to the birth and growth of the United States. It took 14 years for Gutzon Borglum to design and sculpt the 60' granite heads of Presidents Washington, Jefferson, Teddy Roosevelt, and Lincoln. Nearby is a sculpture-in-progress of the Sioux chief, Crazy Horse, riding a snorting horse. At 563' high, it will be the world's largest sculpture. (two words)
6. _____ in Lead is the largest producing underground gold mine in the Western Hemisphere. This mine began in 1876 and is the world's oldest continually operating gold mine.
7. _____ was discovered in the Black Hills in 1874. For two years, prospectors overran the Black Hills, disregarding the sacred lands of the Sioux. The Sioux fought to drive the intruders out in the famous Battle of Little Big Horn in Montana.
8. De Smet is the town that was the setting for the book, *Little Town on the Prairie,* by Laura Ingalls _____. Later she wrote nine Little House books. The De Smet house can be toured by visitors. Each year, De Smet hosts a pageant, performing stories from her books.
10. Custer State Park has one of the world's largest _____ herds.

Down

1. Wind Cave National Monument and _____ Cave were created when water and chemicals seeped into limestone. They are among the world's ten longest caves.
2. The Black Hills got their name because the thick _____ of pine and spruce trees makes the hills look dark from a distance. These dome-shaped hills rise up from the plains. They are really low mountains, 3000-4000' high.
3. _____ Knee Monument is a tribute to those who died when U.S. troops massacred nearly 300 Sioux. It was feared that Sitting Bull would lead an uprising. He was to be arrested, but it turned into a battle and nearly 300 Sioux were killed. This battle ended the fighting between whites and Indians in South Dakota.
5. _____ is a restored mining town that looks like it did in the 1870s. It was the biggest and noisiest milling town in the Black Hills. Wild Bill Hickok was killed while playing poker in a saloon here. He is buried in this town near Calamity Jane, the famous frontierswoman.
9. Badlands National Monument is a land of rugged beauty, full of weird _____ formations and fossil remains. This land has unusual stone towers and cliffs with little plant life, making it seem like the surface of the moon.

© Instructional Fair • TS Denison

41

IF2736 50 States

Tennessee

Volunteer State

Mockingbird

Iris

Fill in the lines with the answers to the questions. Then arrange the answers to fit into the puzzle boxes.

_____ 1. The state's nickname, "Volunteer State," dates back to this war, when the U.S. government gave each state a quota of soldiers to fill. Tennessee swamped recruiting stations with more than 30,000 volunteers.

_____ 2. The TVA (Tennessee Valley Authority) was the agency that constructed many of these on the Tennessee River to provide power for industry and many lakes for recreation and flood control.

_____ 3. The Great Smoky Mountain National Park, part of these mountains, is named for the bluish haze that normally covers them.

_____ 4. Nashville is the world center for this type of music and is the home to the Grand Ole Opry and Opryland, a major concert center.

_____ 5. This national laboratory is where scientists helped build the atomic bomb but where peaceful uses of atomic energy are now being researched. (two words)

_____ 6. She was born in Clarksville, and when she was four, she lost the use of one leg after an illness. She worked hard to walk again and eventually could run fast enough to win three gold medals in the 1960 Olympics.

_____ 7. This man was a bear hunter, frontiersman, soldier, and then a Tennessee Congressman. In Congress, he took an unpopular stand (and was not reelected) when he said that Indians should not be moved off their lands. He went to Texas, where he died at The Alamo.

_____ 8. He was born near Knoxville and joined the navy at the young age of nine, serving under the captain who adopted him. During the War of 1812 at age 12, he commanded a captured ship. Years later he helped the North win the Civil War and became the first U.S. Navy admiral

_____ 9. This type of graceful Tennessee horse, a famous breed of saddle horse, was developed in the state around 1790 and is still raised in the region today

_____ 10. He was a famous movie star and performer of rock 'n' roll, music which he helped make famous. He lived in a large estate called Graceland, which is open to visitors today.

© Instructional Fair • TS Denison

IF2736 50 States

★ Texas ★

Mockingbird — **Lone Star State** — **Bluebonnet**

Write the letter from Column B that most correctly answers the description found in Column A. Note: More choices are given in Column B than will be used for answers.

Column A

_____ 1. In 1901, near Beaumont, this gusher uncovered one of the most productive oil fields in the world, starting oil refineries and petrochemical plants

_____ 2. Found throughout Texas, they are covered with nine thin bony plates joined together to form a kind of armor.

_____ 3. He was born near Stonewall and became the thirtieth president, taking office after the assassination of President John Kennedy in Dallas in 1963.

_____ 4. Started by a steamboat captain with Mexican longhorn cattle, this grew into one of the world's largest cattle ranches.

_____ 5. This east Texas area of forests, vines, and shrubs once hid outlaws and Civil War deserters and today still has black bears, razorback hogs, orchids, 6' ferns, and carnivorous pitcher plants.

_____ 6. The Rio Grande River makes a large curve at this site which showcases bones of the prehistoric pterodactyl, a flying reptile, in this land of mountains, canyons, and deserts.

_____ 7. From Port Arthur, one of the best women athletes in history, excelling in track, golf, swimming, basketball, baseball, football, pocket billiards, some boxing, and track and field at the 1932 Olympic Games

_____ 8. Site of "mission control" for the Mercury, Gemini, and Apollo space flights, plus an astronaut training center located in Houston

_____ 9. Spanish mission in San Antonio where Texans withdrew from the Mexican army in 1836 during the fight for independence. They fought off the Mexicans for 13 days. All Texans were eventually killed, including Davy Crockett.

_____ 10. Country Texas became for about ten years when it broke from Mexico and adopted the flag with one, lone star. It was led by Sam Houston.

Column B

A. Lyndon Baines Johnson Space Center
B. The Spindletop
C. Lone Star State
D. Panhandle
E. Big Bend National Park
F. "Babe" Didrikson Zaharias
G. Republic of Texas
H. Lyndon Baines Johnson
I. George Bush
J. The Alamo
K. King Ranch
L. Armadillos
M. Dallas
N. Barbara Jordan
O. Dwight D. Eisenhower
P. Big Thicket National Preserve
Q. Scott Joplin
R. Tornado Alley
S. Cotton
T. Guadalupe Mountains National
U. Houston Ship Canal

© Instructional Fair • TS Denison

IF2736 50 States

★ Utah ★

Beehive State

Sea gull — *Sego lily*

Fill in the answers to the following questions. A few clues are given.

1. He was the religious leader who led the Mormon pioneers to the Salt Lake Valley from Illinois in 1847 so they could practice their religion without being bothered by others. _ _ _ _ H O _   _ _ _ _ _ _
2. These birds miraculously appeared and ate the swarms of grasshoppers which were destroying the first season of crops of the Mormon settlers. _ _ _ O _ _ L _
3. In 1869 the tracks of the Union Pacific and Central Pacific railroads met at this summit, completing the country's first transcontinental railroad. The last spike driven in the tracks was golden. _ _ _ M _ _ O _ _ _ _
4. In Paiute, the name of Utah's first national park means "red rocks standing like men in a bowl-shaped canyon." _ O _ _ _   _ _ _ _ _ N
5. This open-pit copper mine is the largest in the world. Utah is also rich in coal, gold, silver, lead, and uranium. O _ _ N _ _ _ _ _
6. These mountains run through central Utah and are popular for hiking, camping, and skiing. _ _ _ _ O _ H
7. This area of Salt Lake City is a landscaped park that contains the Mormon Temple and Salt Lake Tabernacle. _ _ _ O _   O _ _ _ R _
8. These salt flats form a hard, smooth, flat desert that is perfect for high-speed auto racing. Drivers attempt to set land speed records here. _ _ N _ O _ _ _ O
9. The Colorado River becomes this lake behind Glen Canyon Dam. Boaters can explore hundreds of side canyons. Above the lake is Rainbow Bridge, the largest natural bridge in the world. _ O _ _   _ _ W _ O _
10. He was born George Leroy Parker in Circleville. He became a noted outlaw who used the Utah canyons as his hideout. His life story became a movie. _ _ _ _ C _   _ O _ _ _ _

Write the letters found in the circles. Unscramble these letters until they provide the answer to the name of the large Utah lake that is eight times saltier than the ocean, where swimmers find that the heavy salt water makes floating easy.

_ _ _ _ _ _   _ _ _ _   _ _ _ _

★ Vermont ★

Green Mountain State

Hermit thrush

Red clover

Locate the answers to the following questions in the word search.

1. When England gained control of Vermont in 1763, the King said Vermont belonged to New York. This upset _____, so he formed the Green Mountain Boys, a loosely knit military group, to defend Vermont's claim to the land. They captured Fort Ticonderoga in New York from the British without a fight. (two words)
2. After Fort Ticonderoga was captured, Vermont became an independent country, and in 1777 adopted a _____ that provided for state education, gave the right of every male to vote, and forbade slavery, which were all firsts in America.
3. At _____ sites in Vermont, granite, slate, and marble are dug out of mountains and used to build magnificent buildings, such as the Lincoln and Jefferson Memorials in Washington, D.C.
4. The _____ Battle Monument is a 306' obelisk honoring the victory of the inexperienced Americans over the British in this Revolutionary War battle. This victory provided hope that the Americans might be able to win the war.
5. Norman _____ lived in Arlington and painted scenes of typical American life. He often used the town in his famous paintings which were shown as cover pictures on the *Saturday Evening Post* magazine.
6. Vermont was named from the French, *vert mont*, or _____. This beautiful land attracts tourists for outdoor activities and to see scenery such as the colorful fall foliage and over 100 covered bridges. (two words)
7. Poet Robert _____ spent part of his life on a Vermont farm; his famous poems often tell of the snowy woods, birch trees, and the natural beauty of the land.
8. When winter turns to spring, the sap in the sugar maple trees begins to rise and millions of trees are "tapped" with little pipes so the sap can drip out. The sap is then boiled to evaporate the water, and then maple _____ can be made.
9. The beautiful 100-mile long Lake _____ was named after the French explorer Samuel de Champlain, who explored the area in 1609. He said he saw a monster lurking in the depths of the lake, and those who claim to have seen it today call it "Champ."
10. Justin Morgan was owed money but took a colt as payment instead. This horse became the father of America's first own breed of horses, the _____ horse.

```
E N O I T U T I T S N O C F N O
H O I M O N T P E L I E R S E A
S N I A T N U O M N E E R G C F
Y T H M L J E T H A N A L L E N
R A S H I P N O T G N I N N E B
U P F O R T M S A R T H U R P A
P Q U A R R Y A R O C K W E L L
B A R R E F B E H M D A I R Y J
E N G L A N D C O C L I D G E M
```

© Instructional Fair • TS Denison   45   IF2736 50 States

VIRGINIA
Old Dominion

Cardinal

Flowering dogwood

Place the answers to the questions in the crossword puzzle.

Across
1. _____ U.S. presidents were born in this state, more than any other state—Washington, Jefferson, Madison, Monroe, Harrison, Tyler, Taylor, and Wilson.
3. Virginia _____ is the state's largest city. It is an oceanside resort with boardwalks, amusement parks, and sandy beaches.
5. Virginia was very involved in the Revolutionary War. Patrick Henry, governor of Virginia, encouraged the state to join the rest of the colonies in the fight against the British. The British surrendered at _____ to General George Washington in 1781.
8. _____ National Park is known for its scenic mountains and valleys. Skyline Drive follows the ridge through forests that are popular for hiking. Skyline and Luray Caverns are nearby.
9. More Civil War battles were fought in Virginia than in any other state. General Robert E. Lee surrendered his Confederate Army to General U.S. Grant in 1865 at the village of _____ Courthouse.
10. Williamsburg is a restored town, built to show what _____ life was like in the seventeenth century. It was reconstructed so "that the future may learn from the past."

4. _____ National Cemetery is the burial site of many Americans, especially military personnel. President John Kennedy is buried there. It is the site of the Tomb of the Unknowns, holding the bodies of unknown American soldiers from four wars.
6. Jamestown was the first _____ English town in America. The Indian princess, Pocahontas, and her father, Chief Powhatan, lived in the area. It was a poor place for the settlers because of unhealthy conditions from the swampy land. Today, the colonial and Powhatan villages are rebuilt.
7. The _____ is a five-sided building in Arlington that is the largest office building in the world. Over 25,000 people work there, mainly for the Department of Defense.

Down
2. Along the Eastern Shore is the annual roundup and pony sale in Chincoteague. These horses are believed to be descended from animals who swam ashore from a sixteenth-century shipwreck. The book by Marguerite ____, *Misty of Chincoteague*, is based on true events.

© Instructional Fair • TS Denison   46   IF2736 50 States

WASHINGTON

Willow goldfinch

Evergreen State

Coast rhododendron

Write the letter from Column B that most correctly answers the description found in Column A. Not all the letters in Column B will be used.

Column A

_____ 1. Largest concrete dam in the United States and one of the greatest sources of water power, is three times as large as the Great Pyramid in Egypt, and its waters help irrigate the dry, eastern side of the state

_____ 2. County that is considered the "Holland in America" because of the many flower bulbs that are grown here, including daffodils and tulips

_____ 3. The Strait of Juan de Fuca connects this deep arm of water with the Pacific Ocean, providing a large natural harbor for ships coming to and from Seattle, Tacoma, and Olympia.

_____ 4. Park-like fairground that was the site of the 1962 Century 21 World's Fair and still has parts remaining such as the monorail, Space Needle, Coliseum, Opera House, and Pacific Science Center

_____ 5. The Seattle area is the location for several of these plants which make aircraft and aerospace equipment. The process is made easier by the great amount of hydroelectric power for the production of aluminum.

_____ 6. The top 1,300' of this blew off when it erupted in 1980, killing about 60 people and countless wildlife and trees and covering the land with gray ash.

_____ 7. Moisture-bearing clouds from the ocean are blocked from blowing east by these mountains, which divide the state into the wet, forested west side and the drier lands in the east.

_____ 8. Land of tall peaks with glaciers, world's greatest variety of giant trees, rain forests, beaches, and much rainfall

_____ 9. From 1836-1847, this mission brought the Christian religion to the Cayuse Indians. It was a welcome resting spot for pioneers heading West.

_____ 10. Washington is the leading producer of this crop for the country, especially the red and golden delicious varieties.

Column B

A. Whatcom
B. Mt. St. Helens
C. Bonnie Dunbar
D. Cascades
E. North Cascades National Park
F. Apples
G. Ginkgo Petrified Forest
H. Seattle Center
I. Lewis and Clark
J. Whitman Mission National Historic Site
K. Spokane
L. San Juan Islands
M. Olympic National Park
N. Grand Coulee Dam
O. Pacific Crest Trail
P. Puget Sound
Q. Bonneville Dam
R. Mt. Rainier
S. Tacoma
T. Point Defiance Park
U. Boeing

★ WEST VIRGINIA ★

Cardinal | Mountain State | Rhododendron

Fill in the lines with the answers to the questions. Then arrange the answers to fit into the puzzle boxes.

_____ 1. Legendary West Virginia railroad tunnel builder who could work faster with a sledgehammer than others could with mechanical drills (two words)

_____ 2. An industry that grew because the state has plenty of fine silica sand, with natural gas to fuel the factory furnaces

_____ 3. West Virginia separated from this state to become a new state in 1863, when West Virginia refused to secede from the Union during the Civil War.

_____ 4. This beautiful mountainous state has little level ground since it is located in these mountains

_____ 5. She was born in West Virginia but as a baby went with her missionary parents to China, where she lived for many years and wrote award-winning books, including *The Good Earth*. (two words)

_____ 6. This U.S. arsenal was stormed by John Brown and others, hoping to steal weapons that they planned to give to slaves to help them gain their freedom. Brown was arrested and hanged. (two words)

_____ 7. One of at least 500 caves in the state, this spectacular one near Lewisburg was where Confederate troops attended church services underground during the Civil War. (two words)

_____ 8. This natural resource is found under half of the state, and an explanation of its mining technology and procedures is shown to tourists at the Beckley Exhibition

_____ 9. The mountains have many of these mineral resorts, known as medicine water by the Indians because of their health-giving properties. These were also popular during colonial days, even with George Washington.

_____ 10. In 1884, Sulphur Springs was the site of the first of these recreational areas in the United States. (two words)

© Instructional Fair • TS Denison   48   IF2736 50 States

★ WISCONSIN ★
Badger State

Robin — Wood violet

Fill in the lines with the answers to the questions. Then arrange the answers to fit into the puzzle boxes.

_____ 1. When this crop declined due to overuse of the land, many farmers switched to the raising of dairy cattle. Now Wisconsin is a leader in the production of milk and cheese.

_____ 2. The Badger State originally did not get its name from the animal but, instead, from the miners of this metal who lived underground in dugout homes.

_____ 3. Frank Lloyd Wright was one of America's most famous of these, who designed his summer home, Taliesein, in Spring Green, and successfully designed the Imperial Hotel in Tokyo, Japan, to withstand earthquakes.

_____ 4. These five brothers began giving shows with farm animals and eventually added tents and formed their own circus, which became the largest in the world.

_____ 5. These Dells are a scenic area where the Wisconsin River carved canyons, cliffs, and unusual rock formations. Visitors ride in amphibious trucks called "ducks" that drive into the river for floating tours.

_____ 6. Some say this steam-driven car called the "Spark," invented by this doctor in 1873, was the first true car.

_____ 7. Margarethe Schurz opened the first of these in the nation in Watertown; it was based on models from Germany

_____ 8. Ehrich Weiss, a native of Wisconsin, later took the name Harry Houdini and became a famous one of these. He was known for his amazing escapes, such as from a locked box that was dropped into a river.

_____ 9. This bird named "Old Abe" was taken to the Civil War as a mascot by Wisconsin soldiers. This resulted in many stories of his narrow escapes in battle and of the encouragement he gave the soldiers as he flew overhead during battles.

_____ 10. In Wisconsin, a land with many forests, tall tales were told of this lumberjack whose footprints were said to have formed Wisconsin's many lakes (which were actually caused by glaciers). (two words)

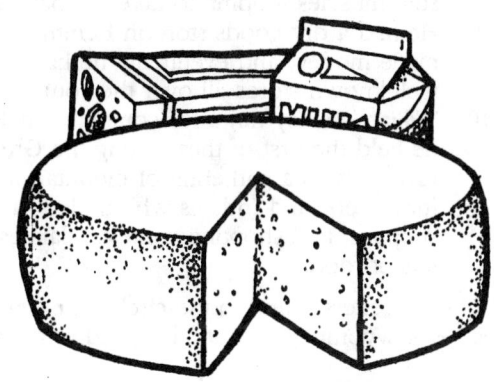

© Instructional Fair • TS Denison   49   IF2736 50 States

★ WYOMING ★

Meadowlark

Equality State

Indian paintbrush

Fill in the answers to the following questions. A few clues are given.

1. Wyoming has many miles of this trail and its historic sites, a few of which include Fort Laramie, Register Cliff, Independence Rock, Fort Casper, and Fort Laramie.
   _ _ (_) _ _ (_) _ _ I _

2. Wyoming has been progressive in women's rights. Women were given the right to vote in 1869, the first in the country. This lady was the first woman governor in the United States.
   _ _ _ _ _ _ (_) _ S _

3. This was the first national park in the United States. It is known for its 10,000 geysers, hot springs, fossil forests, canyons, waterfalls, and wildlife.
   _ _ L _ _ _ _ _ _ (_) _

4. Since the state's soil is poor, much of the land is used for this type of ranching. Cowboys also work at dude ranches, which are resorts that offer tourists a flavor of ranch life.
   _ _ _ (_) _ E _

5. This was the nation's first national monument. It is a huge volcanic rock column, nearly as tall as Sears Tower in Chicago.
   (_) _ _ _ _ ' S _ _ _ _ _

6. He holds the record for the longest Pony Express ride. When he was 15, he rode 322 miles because his replacement had been killed. He killed many buffalo to feed men building the railroads.
   _ _ _ _ (_) _ _ _ _ _ _
   _ _ D _

7. Ralph Herrick of Douglas made up stories about this mythical Wyoming animal. It is supposed to have a rabbit's body and an antelope's antlers.
   _ _ _ _ _ _ P (_)

8. This natural resource is very important to Wyoming. Explorers and fur trappers found it oozing from the ground and smeared it on sore muscles, hoping to take the pain away.
   (_) _ I _

9. He had a dry goods store in Kemmerer. It made money, and eventually he had well-known stores all over the country.
   _ _ _ _ (_) _ _ _ _ H
   _ _ _ _

10. William Ashley ran a fur company. In 1825, he held the first of these along the Green River. It was a gathering of mountain men, fur traders, and Indians who traded furs and supplies, had shooting contests, dances, and lots of food.
    _ _ (_) _ _ _ _ _ U _

Write the letters found in the circles. Unscramble these letters until they provide the answer to the name of Wyoming's beautiful rugged mountains that were discovered and named by the French.

_ _ _ _ _ _   _ _ _ _ _

WASHINGTON, D.C.

Wood thrush | **Nation's Capital** | American beauty rose

Write the letter from Column B that most correctly answers the description found in Column A. Note: More choices are given in Column B than will be used for answers.

Column A

_____ 1. Most visited museum in the world, containing the *Kitty Hawk*, *Spirit of St. Louis*, and a replica of the space shuttle *Columbia*

_____ 2. In 1912, this country sent Washington, D.C., cherry trees which are planted along the Tidal Basin and are known for their beautiful spring flowers.

_____ 3. Important government papers, such as the original Constitution and Declaration of Independence, are stored here.

_____ 4. Washington, D.C., was named for these people.

_____ 5. Government building where Congress (Senate and House of Representatives) meets to pass the nation's laws

_____ 6. Honors the president who saved the United States during the Civil War and was the site where Martin Luther King, Jr., delivered his famous "I Have A Dream" speech in 1963 during the March on Washington.

_____ 7. Plays, dance programs, concerts, and operas are performed in this building, named in the memory of this president who was assassinated in Texas in 1963.

_____ 8. Building that deals with the solving of certain crimes and provides fascinating tours showing forgery detection, sharp-shooting demonstrations, and much more

_____ 9. Building where the nation's paper money and postage stamps are printed

_____ 10. Shiny, V-shaped black granite wall that honors the men and women who served in one of our country's longest wars. It lists over 58,000 names of the dead or missing.

Column B

A. National Zoo
B. France
C. Lincoln Memorial
D. Vietnam Veterans Memorial
E. National Archives
F. Jefferson Memorial
G. Bureau of Engraving and Printing
H. Kennedy Center for the Performing Arts
I. Japan
J. National Air and Space Museum
K. Capitol
L. George Washington and Christopher Columbus
M. L'Enfant, Ellicott, and Bannecker
N. Federal Bureau of Investigation
O. Washington Monument
P. Galludet College

★ U.S. Dependencies ★
Caribbean

In addition to the 50 states and the District of Columbia which make up the United States, there are also U.S. Dependencies in the Caribbean and Pacific. They come under U.S. protection and receive financial and military assistance, and many of the people are U.S. citizens.

Fill in the answers to the following questions. A few clues are given.

1. Puerto Rico is believed to be the only part of the United States where this Spanish explorer set foot. In 1493, the island was inhabited by the Arawak people. _ _ _ ◯ M _ _ _ _
2. The U.S. Virgin Islands were purchased from Denmark in 1917 for $25 million. This other country claims the other six islands. _ _ _ _ _ T ◯ R _ _ _ _
3. The United States took control of Puerto Rico from this country after the Spanish-American War of 1898. _ P _ ◯ _
4. This outstanding Puerto Rican baseball player won the National League batting championship four times before he died in a plane crash, carrying relief supplies to earthquake victims in Nicaragua. _ _ O _ _ _ _ _
5. The U.S. Virgin Islands average 45" of this each year, but water is scarce. By law, each house must have a cistern to collect water that runs off the roof. During droughts, water must be brought from Puerto Rico. _ _ _ ◯ _ _ _ _
6. Puerto Rico is now a U.S. Commonwealth, but it used to have this political status with the United States. ◯ _ _ _ _ _ L _
7. This national park, found in the U.S. Virgin Islands, is underwater. Five types of coral are found here, plus turtles, sponges, eels, sea urchins, fish, whales, and dolphins. ◯ _ R _ _ _ _ _ ◯
8. This island is located between Jamaica and Haiti. It is uninhabited but used as a lighthouse under the administration of the U.S. Coast Guard. _ _ _ ◯ _ N _
9. The first Spanish settlement on Puerto Rico was built in 1509 after this explorer conquered the island. He looked at the harbor and named the island Puerto Rico, meaning "rich port." _ _ _ ◯ _ S _
10. Many of the U.S. Virgin Island descendants were brought to the islands by Europeans. They were brought as these, people owned by others and forced to work against their will. _ ◯ _ _ _ _ _ E _ ◯

_ _ ◯ _ _ S _

Write the letters found in the circles. Unscramble these letters until they provide the answer to the name of the naval base the U.S. leases in Cuba.

_ _ _ _ _ _ _ _ _ _ _

★ U.S. Dependencies ★
Pacific

After World War II, some Pacific islands were placed in America's care by the United Nations. Others had been part of the nation for many years before that. They are unincorporated U.S. territories, U.S. commonwealths, or U.N. trust territories/U.S. administered.

Locate the answers to the following questions in the word search.

1. Residents of _____ are considered American nationals but not citizens and cannot vote in U.S. elections. They have a delegate to Congress who can vote only in committees. (two words)
2. Guam is the largest and most southern of the _____ Islands in the West Pacific but is not part of the political unit of these islands.
3. Palau, consisting of 200 of the _____ Islands, has recovered from near-total destruction from the bombing raids of World War II.
4. American Samoa is the only U.S. territory in the _____ Hemisphere.
5. During the invasion of Guam by American planes in World War II, nearly all of the island's _____ were killed. Now, however, several species are making a comeback, particularly kingfishers and fruit doves.
6. The United States airplanes that dropped atomic bombs during World War II on Hiroshima and Nagasaki, Japan, in 1945 took off from the island of _____ in the Commonwealth of the Northern Mariana Islands.
7. _____ is considered the island "Where America's Day Begins" because it lies west of the International Date Line.
8. American Samoa is made up of six islands that are actually _____ peaks rising from the ocean floor.
9. It is very damp in Guam due to the high _____, so residents use electric heaters to dry closets and electric blankets to prevent mildew in beds.
10. _____ Island was used by the U.S. military during World War II, as an air and submarine base. Later, it was used as a stopover during the Vietnam War; it was also a temporary camp for thousands of Vietnamese refugees on their way to the United States.

```
K S A A A E Y S A I P A N M V
O O G N T A G T I N I A N A O
R C A A O S D R I B S E A R L
O A N I L T A I E D N E W S C
R R A R L O O K J F I N M H A
A O M A S N A C I R E M A A N
J L C M O W P A G O P A U L I
I I U S O U T H E R N S G H C
M N P O L Y N E S I A N I W O
A E H O W L A N D M I D W A Y
```

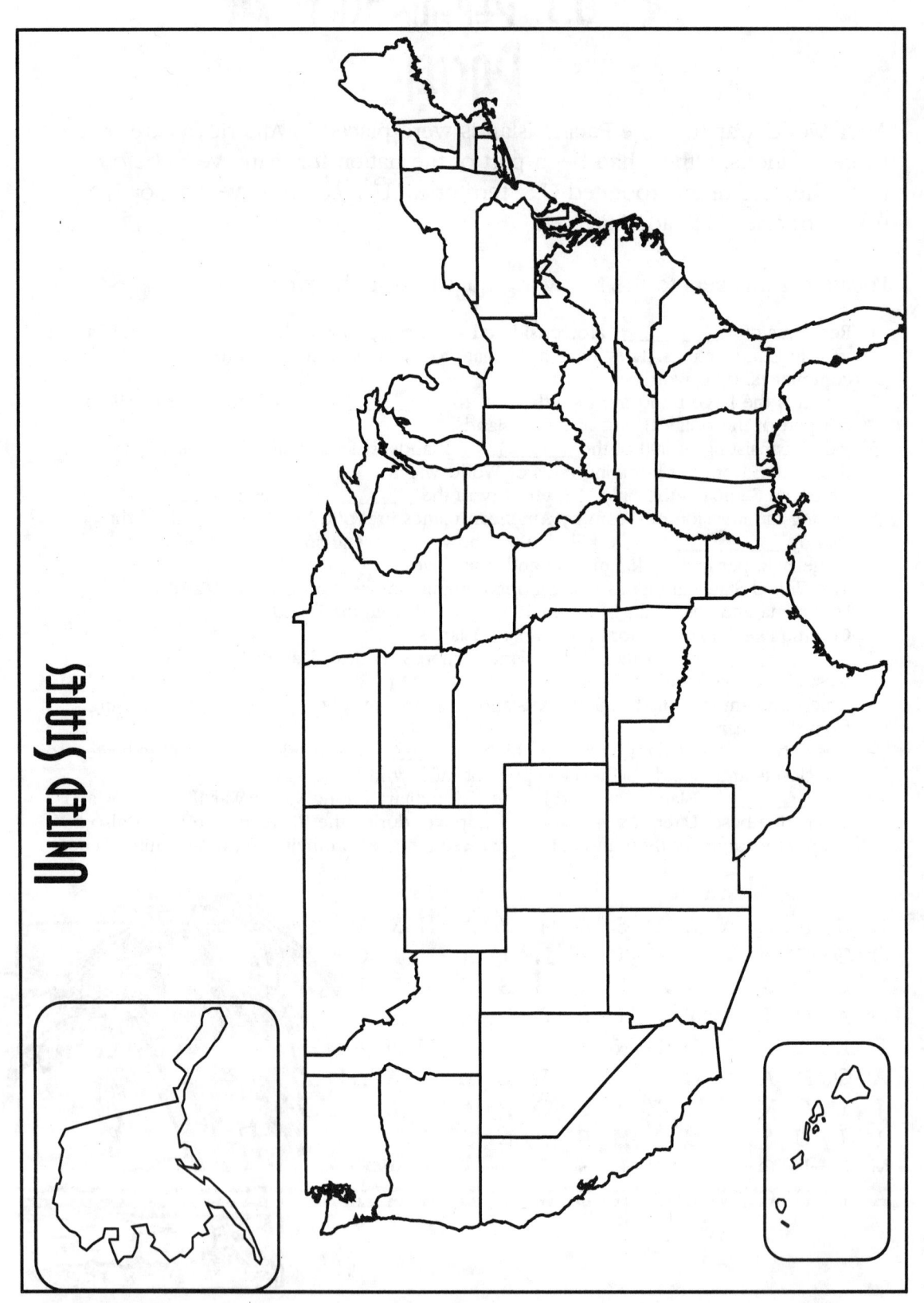

United States

54

U.S. Dependencies

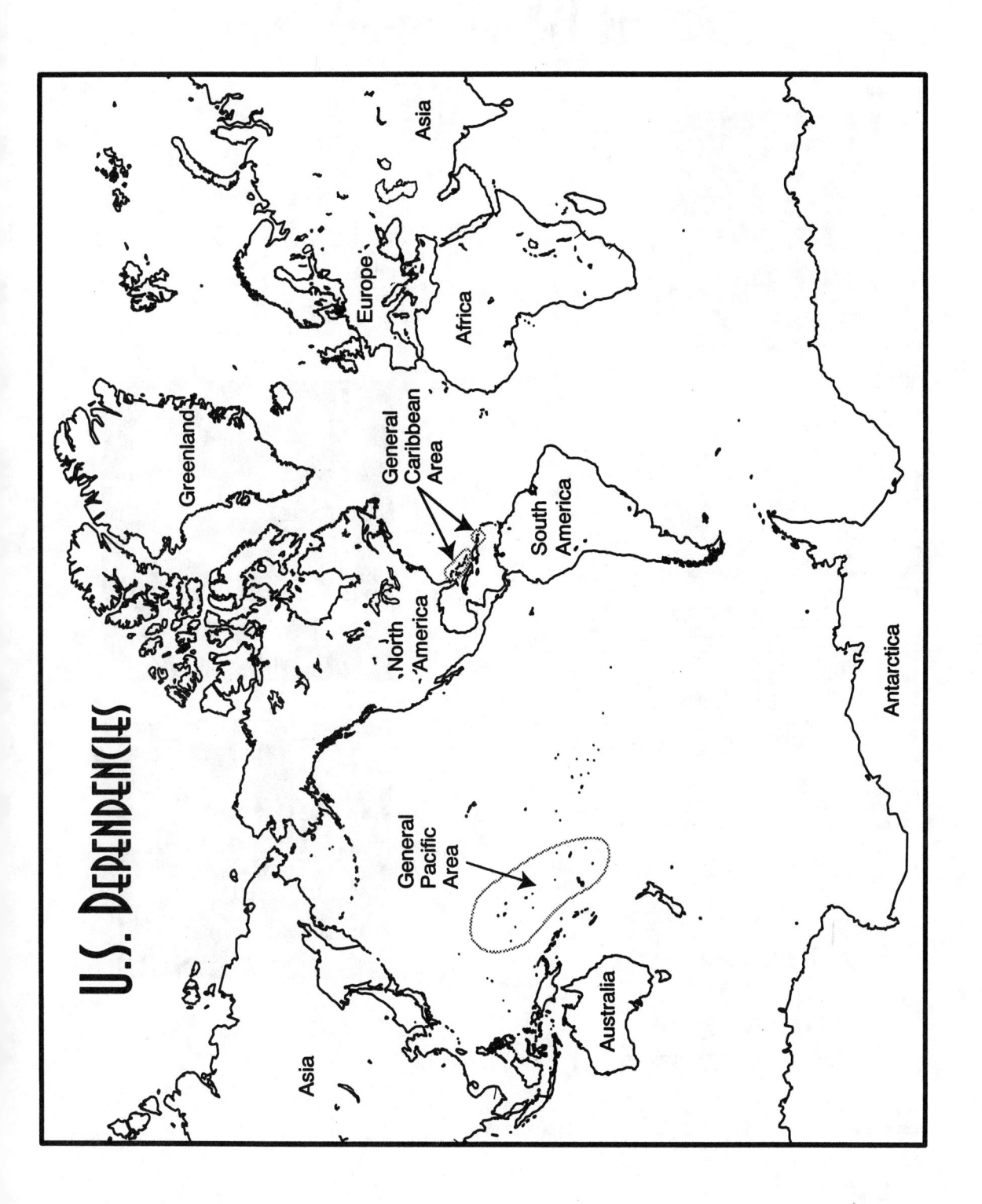

- Asia
- Europe
- Africa
- Greenland
- General Caribbean Area
- North America
- South America
- Antarctica
- General Pacific Area
- Australia
- Asia

★ Answer Key ★

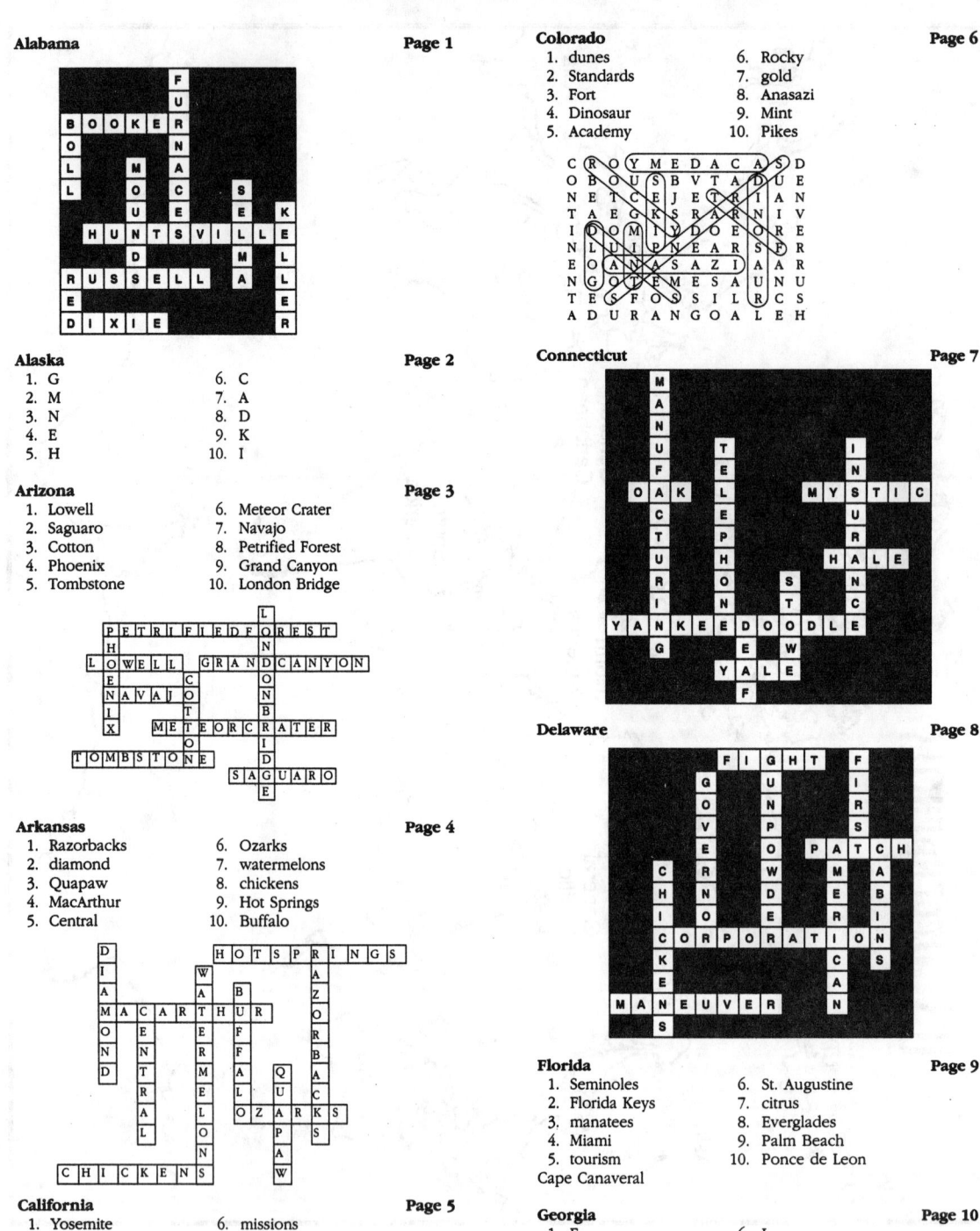

Alabama — Page 1

Colorado — Page 6
1. dunes
2. Standards
3. Fort
4. Dinosaur
5. Academy
6. Rocky
7. gold
8. Anasazi
9. Mint
10. Pikes

Alaska — Page 2
1. G
2. M
3. N
4. E
5. H
6. C
7. A
8. D
9. K
10. I

Connecticut — Page 7

Arizona — Page 3
1. Lowell
2. Saguaro
3. Cotton
4. Phoenix
5. Tombstone
6. Meteor Crater
7. Navajo
8. Petrified Forest
9. Grand Canyon
10. London Bridge

Delaware — Page 8

Arkansas — Page 4
1. Razorbacks
2. diamond
3. Quapaw
4. MacArthur
5. Central
6. Ozarks
7. watermelons
8. chickens
9. Hot Springs
10. Buffalo

Florida — Page 9
1. Seminoles
2. Florida Keys
3. manatees
4. Miami
5. tourism
6. St. Augustine
7. citrus
8. Everglades
9. Palm Beach
10. Ponce de Leon

Cape Canaveral

California — Page 5
1. Yosemite
2. Death Valley
3. gold rush
4. La Brea
5. bristlecone
6. missions
7. Silicon
8. agriculture
9. Monterey
10. San Francisco

San Andreas Fault

Georgia — Page 10
1. E
2. G
3. L
4. N
5. D
6. J
7. A
8. M
9. C
10. H

© Instructional Fair • TS Denison

IF2736 50 States

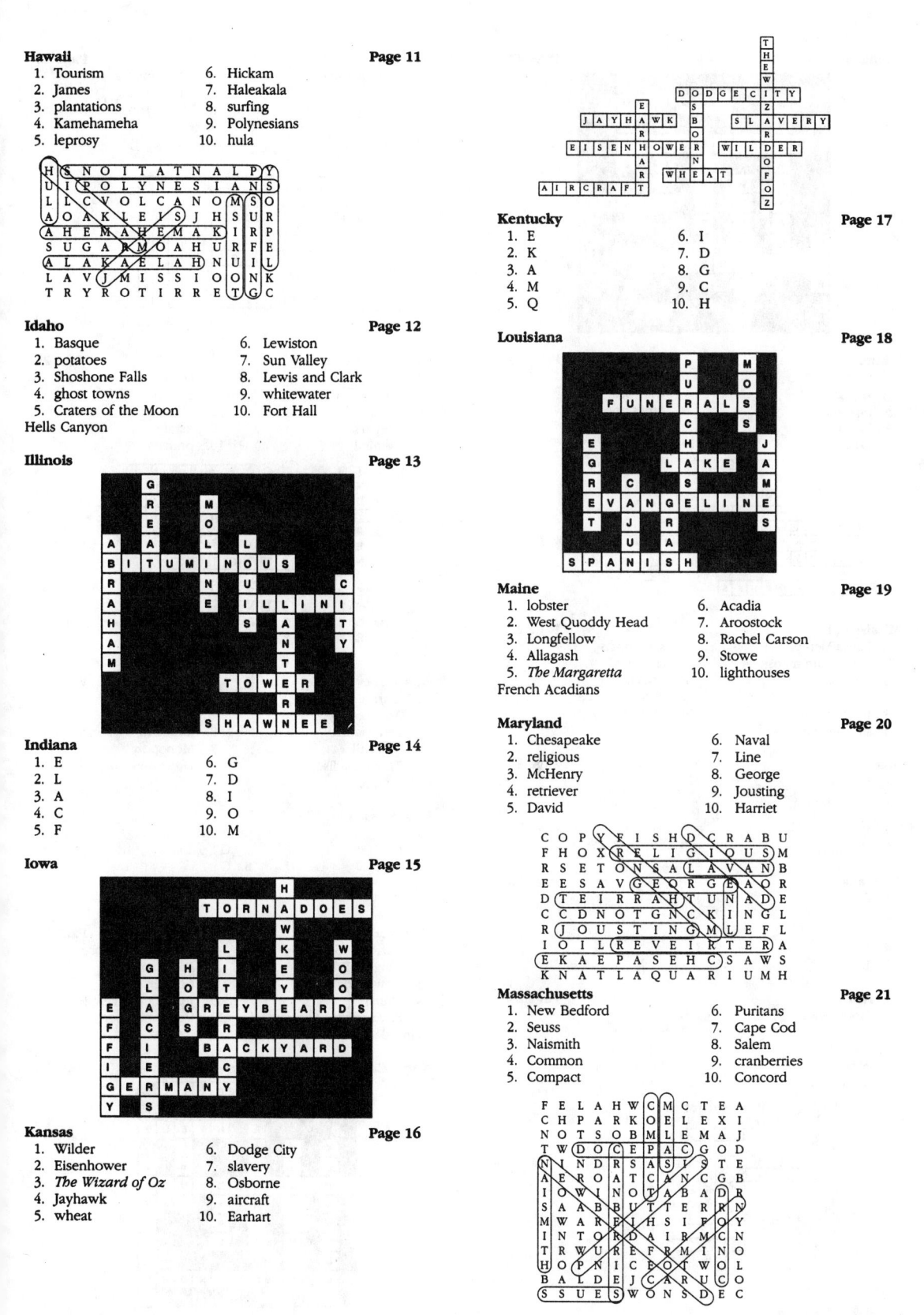

Hawaii — Page 11
1. Tourism
2. James
3. plantations
4. Kamehameha
5. leprosy
6. Hickam
7. Haleakala
8. surfing
9. Polynesians
10. hula

Idaho — Page 12
1. Basque
2. potatoes
3. Shoshone Falls
4. ghost towns
5. Craters of the Moon
6. Lewiston
7. Sun Valley
8. Lewis and Clark
9. whitewater
10. Fort Hall

Hells Canyon

Illinois — Page 13

Indiana — Page 14
1. E
2. L
3. A
4. C
5. F
6. G
7. D
8. I
9. O
10. M

Iowa — Page 15

Kansas — Page 16
1. Wilder
2. Eisenhower
3. *The Wizard of Oz*
4. Jayhawk
5. wheat
6. Dodge City
7. slavery
8. Osborne
9. aircraft
10. Earhart

Kentucky — Page 17
1. E
2. K
3. A
4. M
5. Q
6. I
7. D
8. G
9. C
10. H

Louisiana — Page 18

Maine — Page 19
1. lobster
2. West Quoddy Head
3. Longfellow
4. Allagash
5. *The Margaretta*
6. Acadia
7. Aroostock
8. Rachel Carson
9. Stowe
10. lighthouses

French Acadians

Maryland — Page 20
1. Chesapeake
2. religious
3. McHenry
4. retriever
5. David
6. Naval
7. Line
8. George
9. Jousting
10. Harriet

Massachusetts — Page 21
1. New Bedford
2. Seuss
3. Naismith
4. Common
5. Compact
6. Puritans
7. Cape Cod
8. Salem
9. cranberries
10. Concord

© Instructional Fair • TS Denison IF2736 50 States

Michigan — Page 22

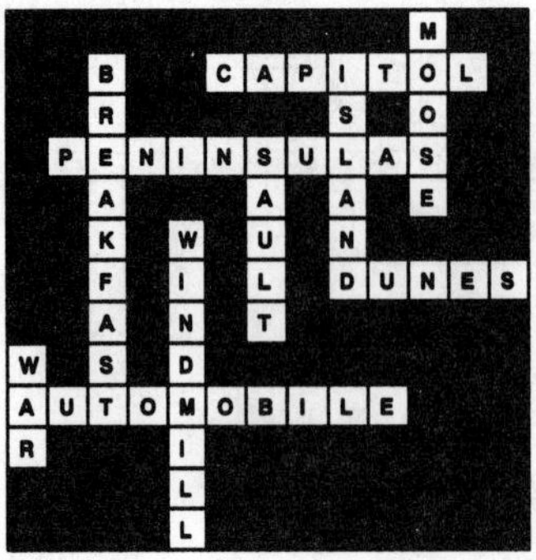

Minnesota — Page 23
1. iron ore
2. voyageurs
3. pipestone
4. Itaska
5. canoe
6. glaciers
7. wild rice
8. runestone
9. peat
10. Peanuts

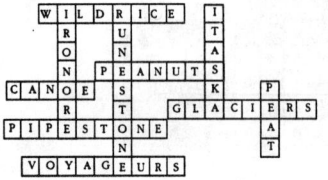

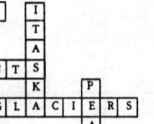

Mississippi — Page 24
1. James Meredith
2. antebellum mansions
3. Vicksburg
4. Biloxi
5. Jim Henson
6. showboats
7. catfish
8. Choctaw
9. Natchez Trace
10. Memorial Day

William Faulkner

Missouri — Page 25
1. J
2. F
3. Q
4. K
5. N
6. M
7. C
8. B
9. E
10. G

Montana — Page 26
1. F
2. K
3. M
4. D
5. E
6. J
7. Q
8. H
9. L
10. A

Nebraska — Page 27
1. Homestead
2. sod
3. football
4. Arbor Day
5. Wild West
6. Agate
7. Strategic
8. Oglala
9. Boys Town
10. Cather

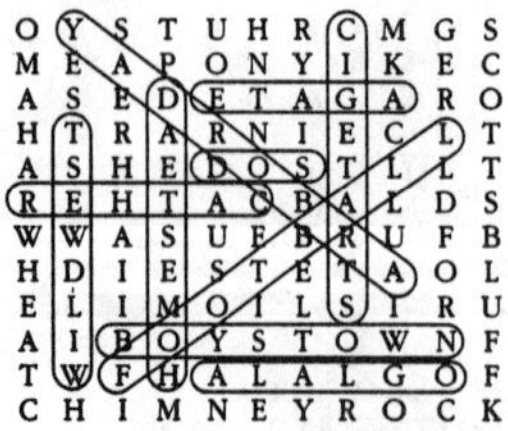

Nevada — Page 28
1. Virginia City
2. Comstock Lode
3. Las Vegas
4. Hoover
5. Tahoe
6. Winnemucca
7. Great Basin
8. Thompson
9. Frémont
10. camels

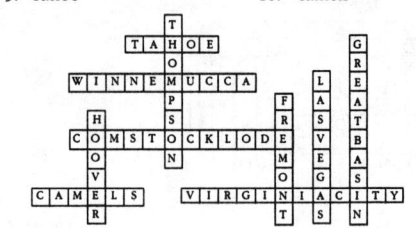

New Hampshire — Page 29
1. Hale
2. Cog
3. White
4. Shepard
5. Admiral
6. velocity
7. Shaker
8. Mountain
9. textile
10. primary

New Jersey — Page 30
1. Clara Barton
2. Atlantic City
3. hadrasaurus
4. baseball
5. Thomas Edison
6. cranberries
7. manufacturing
8. farmland
9. Monopoly
10. Great Swamp

Hindenburg

New Mexico — Page 31
1. F
2. O
3. M
4. I
5. Q
6. A
7. G
8. C
9. K
10. E

New York — Page 32
1. Elizabeth Stanton
2. Niagara Falls
3. New York City
4. Dutch
5. St. Lawrence Seaway
6. Franklin D. Roosevelt
7. Erie Canal
8. Cooperstown
9. John D. Rockefeller
10. Statue of Liberty

Adirondack

North Carolina — Page 33

© Instructional Fair • TS Denison

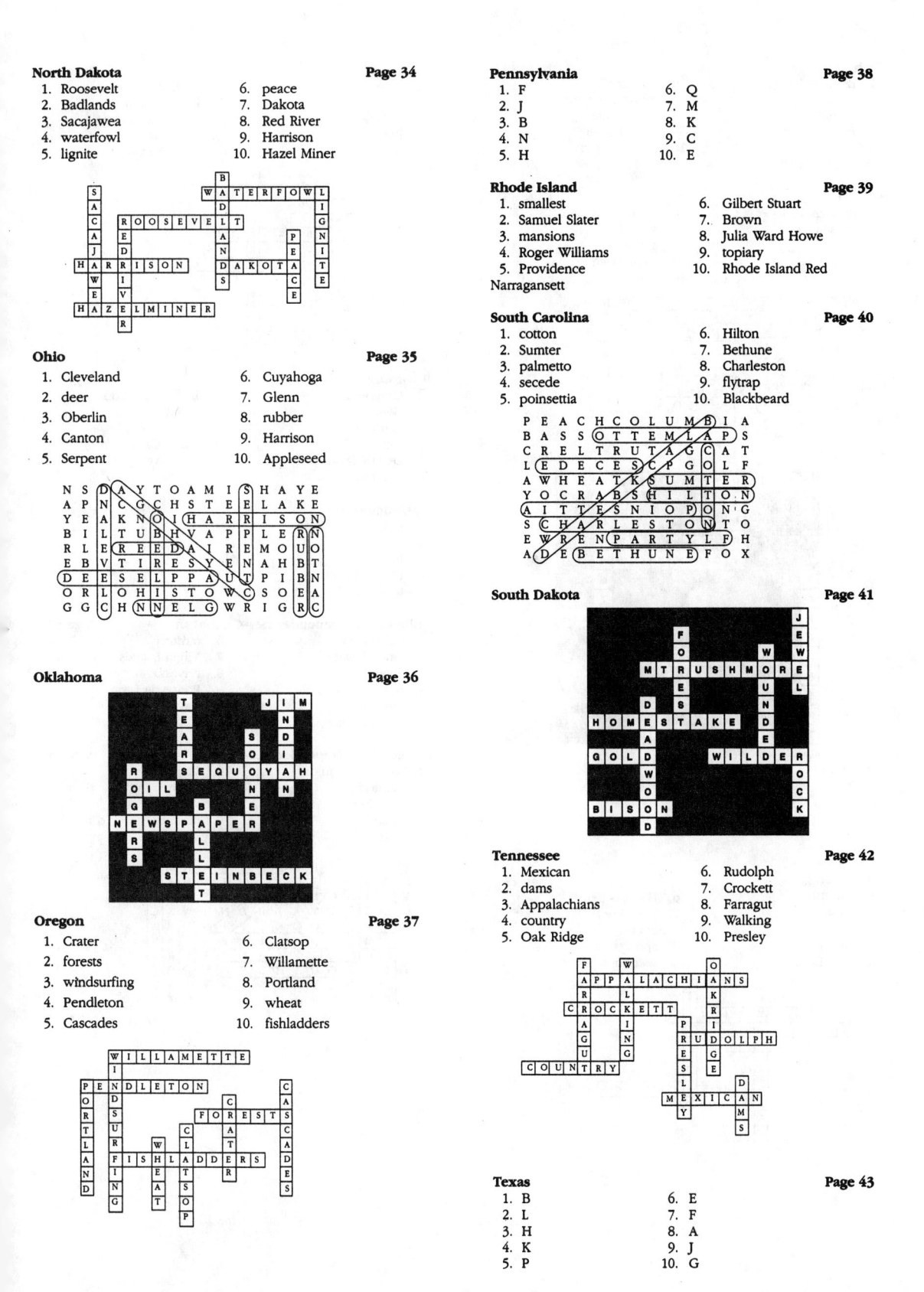

North Dakota — Page 34
1. Roosevelt
2. Badlands
3. Sacajawea
4. waterfowl
5. lignite
6. peace
7. Dakota
8. Red River
9. Harrison
10. Hazel Miner

Ohio — Page 35
1. Cleveland
2. deer
3. Oberlin
4. Canton
5. Serpent
6. Cuyahoga
7. Glenn
8. rubber
9. Harrison
10. Appleseed

Oklahoma — Page 36

Oregon — Page 37
1. Crater
2. forests
3. windsurfing
4. Pendleton
5. Cascades
6. Clatsop
7. Willamette
8. Portland
9. wheat
10. fishladders

Pennsylvania — Page 38
1. F
2. J
3. B
4. N
5. H
6. Q
7. M
8. K
9. C
10. E

Rhode Island — Page 39
1. smallest
2. Samuel Slater
3. mansions
4. Roger Williams
5. Providence Narragansett
6. Gilbert Stuart
7. Brown
8. Julia Ward Howe
9. topiary
10. Rhode Island Red

South Carolina — Page 40
1. cotton
2. Sumter
3. palmetto
4. secede
5. poinsettia
6. Hilton
7. Bethune
8. Charleston
9. flytrap
10. Blackbeard

South Dakota — Page 41

Tennessee — Page 42
1. Mexican
2. dams
3. Appalachians
4. country
5. Oak Ridge
6. Rudolph
7. Crockett
8. Farragut
9. Walking
10. Presley

Texas — Page 43
1. B
2. L
3. H
4. K
5. P
6. E
7. F
8. A
9. J
10. G

© Instructional Fair • TS Denison

IF2736 50 States

Utah   Page 44
1. Brigham Young   6. Wasatch
2. seagulls   7. Temple Square
3. Promontory   8. Bonneville
4. Bryce Canyon   9. Lake Powell
5. Kennecott   10. Butch Cassidy

Great Salt Lake

Vermont   Page 45
1. Ethan Allen   6. Green Mountains
2. constitution   7. Frost
3. quarry   8. syrup
4. Bennington   9. Champlain
5. Rockwell   10. Morgan

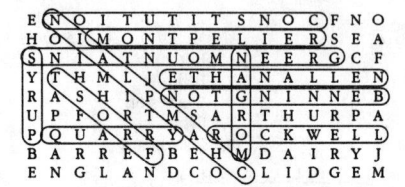

Virginia   Page 46

Washington   Page 47
1. N   6. B
2. A   7. D
3. P   8. M
4. H   9. J
5. U   10. F

West Virginia   Page 48
1. John Henry   6. Harpers Ferry
2. glass   7. Lost World
3. Virginia   8. coal
4. Allegheny   9. springs
5. Pearl Buck   10. golf courses

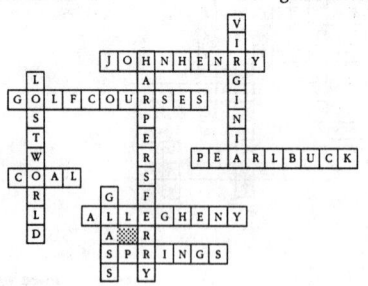

Wisconsin   Page 49
1. wheat   6. Carhart
2. lead   7. kindergarten
3. architects   8. magician
4. Ringling   9. eagle
5. Wisconsin   10. Paul Bunyan

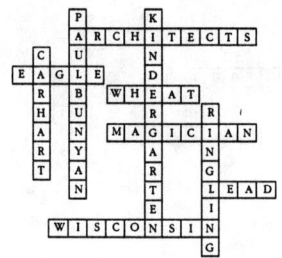

Wyoming   Page 50
1. Oregon Trail   6. Buffalo Bill Cody
2. Nellie Ross   7. jackalope
3. Yellowstone   8. oil
4. cattle   9. James Cash Penney
5. Devil's Tower   10. rendezvous

Grand Tetons

Washington, D.C.   Page 51
1. J   6. C
2. I   7. H
3. E   8. N
4. L   9. G
5. K   10. D

United States Dependencies–Caribbean   Page 52
1. Columbus   6. territory
2. Great Britain   7. Virgin Islands
3. Spain   8. Navassa
4. Roberto Clemente   9. Ponce de Leon
5. rainfall   10. slaves

Guantánamo Bay

United States Dependencies–Pacific   Page 53
1. American Samoa   6. Tinian
2. Mariana   7. Guam
3. Caroline   8. volcanic
4. Southern   9. humidity
5. birds   10. Wake

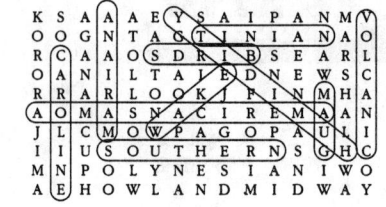